Quality-Aware Tooling

Inauguraldissertation
der Philosophisch-naturwissenschaftlichen Fakultät
der Universität Bern

vorgelegt von

Yuriy Tymchuk

von Ukraine

Leiter der Arbeit:
Prof. Dr. O. Nierstrasz
Institut für Informatik
Universität Bern

ISBN: 978-0-244-65026-1
First edition, November 2017

Acknowledgements

While this dissertation is just one small step for mankind, it is one giant leap for me. I sincerely thank everyone who supported me on this journey. Although it is nearly impossible to mention every individual who contributed to my Ph.D. experience, I will do my best in the following acknowledgments.

First of all, I want to express my gratitude to Oscar Nierstrasz who gave me an opportunity to work at the Software Composition Group in gorgeous Bern and who saved my doctoral studies. I thank him for his patience and tolerance for my mistakes, proofreading the papers that had to be ready "for yesterday," and for the guidance on my Ph.D. trail. I will always admire the way Oscar managed to organize the work in our group and keep track of everything possible. I am going to miss the coffee-break puzzles and the rubber chicken.

I am grateful to Radu Marinescu for accepting to be on my Ph.D. committee and for reviewing this dissertation. I thank Paolo Favaro for accepting to chair the examination.

I was lucky to spend a couple of years surrounded by smart, fun and friendly members of the Software Composition Group. Big thanks to Andrei for inspiring me with his work and his thesis, Jan for discussing exciting ideas (and letting me know that my Google calendar issue will not be fixed), and Boris for inserting fun transitions between my context switches. Thank you, Manuel, for building Randi, supervising Radi, being a great travel companion, and proofreading this dissertation in a turbo-mode. I am grateful to Nevena who is always caring when it comes to important matters, and for mindful discussions especially the ones over a glass of sangria. I thank Claudio for teaching me how to interact with *the Switzerland*, Leonel for various parenting ideas, and Mohammad for proving that a deadline of 15 minutes is not dead enough. I also thank Andrea for leaving the git server in an adequate state, Pascal for the fresh ideas that he brought to the group, and Oli for sharing his DIY experience during coffee breaks. I want to express my gratitude to Haidar for giving me a master class of applying for apartments in Bern, giving away lots of baby stuff, recommending me for a new job, and always sharing new swiss life hacks.

I also want to thank David, Kevin, Lars, and Radi for the work that we did together and their technical assistance.

I thank Iris for helping me to get an apartment, organizing friendly events, and solving plenty of my problems, many of which I did not even know about. I thank Bettina for taking care of my ever-changing contract extensions and for helping me to organize the defense.

My Ph.D. journey did not start in Bern though. I am grateful to Michele Lanza for inviting me to the sunny Lugano and supervising my doctoral research. I will always remember the strict presentation rehearsals, writing of the best abstracts in the world, and Fantozzi quotes during the coffee breaks. I want to thank the whole Lugano team: Andrea for involuntarily appearing in the fun photos that I took (and for guidance in my research), Luca for teaching me Italian and learning Ukrainian from me, Roberto for sharing the sense of beauty in technology, and Tommaso for being a good friend. I want to especially thank all the Italians with whom I worked for inspiring me to improve my culinary skills. Who knows how often I am going to benefit from my Ph.D. diploma, but I can always eat a tasty pasta or a delicious tiramisu.

I would not have gone this path if Stephane Ducasse did not invite me to his research group for an internship. I thank him for always staying in touch, working with other Ukrainian students, teaching in Ukrainian universities and regularly brainstorming on the future projects. I also appreciate the help and guidance of Nicolas Anquetil and Anne Etien.

I thank the people from Smalltalk and Pharo communities with whom I tightly interacted during the last few years. I am especially grateful to Tudor Girba, Marcus Denker, Esteban Lorenzano, Clement Bera, Alexandre Bergel, Gustavo Santos, Dale Henrichs, Aliaksei Syrel, Max Leske, Guillermo Polito, Stephan Eggermont, Tim McKinnon and others with whom I programmed, brainstormed, or simply went out for a beer.

I am grateful to the APPS Faculty of the Ukrainian Catholic University for keeping a part my consciousness in my homeland. I thank Yaroslav Prytula for warmly welcoming me every time I visit Lviv, and for the engaging discussions over an aromatic cup coffee. I thank Oleksii Molchanovskyi for giving me an opportunity to teach in the master program for data scientists and for sharing new ideas about education. I am grateful to Myroslava Romaniuk who doubtlessly programmed day and night to release a new version of Renraku. I thank Oleksandr Zaytsev who appeared out of nowhere, started to build cool projects, and organized a Ukrainian Smalltalk Users Group in Lviv.

I am sincerely grateful for all the aid of that my extended family provided over the course of my Ph.D. studies. Some family members understood me, and some did not. Some of them agreed with me, and the others did not. But they believed in me, supported me, and prayed for me. I am especially grateful to my parents who gave me a fantastic start in this life and raised me stubborn enough to survive the Ph.D. experience.

Finally, I want to thank my wife who proofread my papers, reviewed my slides, challenged my ideas, prepared tasty lunches, and said "Everything is going to be good" while hugging me at the end of a long day. I thank you, Natalia, for your unconditional love that made me move forward and create without limits. This dissertation could never happen without you.

There is one more person. My daughter joined me during my doctoral studies and immediately entered most of the activities of our family. Sophia, I thank you for falling asleep on my chest, stubbornly proposing edits to this dissertation, and teaching me more and more every single day. You are not going to remember the presentations that I rehearsed in front of you when you will learn to speak, and I have removed all the characters that you typed into my manuscripts. Nevertheless, you have changed me, and there is a part of you in this book as well.

Yuriy Tymchuk
November 21, 2017

To Natalia and Sophia who always support my crazy ideas and continue loving me.

Наталі та Софії, які завжди підтримують мої шалені ідеї та продовжують мене любити.

Abstract

Programming is a fascinating activity that can yield results capable of changing people lives by automating daily tasks or even completely reimagining how we perform certain activities. Such a great power comes with a handful of challenges, with software maintainability being one of them. Maintainability cannot be validated by executing the program but has to be assessed by analyzing the codebase. This tedious task can be also automated by the means of software development. Programs called static analyzers can process source code and try to detect suspicious patterns. While these programs were proven to be useful, there is also an evidence that they are not used in practice.

In this dissertation we discuss the concept of quality-aware tooling — an approach that seeks a promotion of static analysis by seamlessly integrating it into development tools. We describe our experience of applying quality-aware tooling on a core distribution of a development environment. Our main focus is to provide live quality feedback in the code editor, but we also integrate static analysis into other tools based on our code quality model. We analyzed the attitude of the developers towards the integrated static analysis and assessed the impact of the integration on the development ecosystem.

As a result 90% of software developers find the live feedback useful, quality rules received an overhaul to better match the contemporary development practices, and some developers even experimented with a custom analysis implementations. We discovered that live feedback helped developers to avoid dangerous mistakes, saved time, and taught valuable concepts. But most importantly we changed the developers' attitude towards static analysis from viewing it as just another tool to seeing it as an integral part of their toolset.

Contents

Introduction

People have always tried to assign some meaning of quality to things that matter to them and software is not an exception. During the software crisis of the 1970s Boehm *et al.* identified two main parts of quality: *usability* and *maintainability* [Boehm et al. 1976]. The former concerns how software complies to its functional requirements, whether it is reliable, how efficient it is, *etc.* The latter reflects how the software itself is designed, how complex it is to understand, test, and modify the software. The concept of maintainability highlights that it is not enough to build a project with a rich functionality, but the implementation itself plays a crucial part of the quality rating. Nowadays the ISO 25010 standard of systems and software quality requirements and evaluation defines eight top-level categories including maintainability [ISO/IEC 2010].

Functional requirements can be easily validated by quality assurance engineers or by automated tests. On the other hand, maintainability requires analysis of source code and reasoning about the implementation to identify possible issues based on the prior experience of the analyst. The process of reading code to ensure its quality was first formalized as software inspections by Michael Fagan [Fagan 1976]. Later, the SmartBear[*] software company revealed how code reviews can protect projects from $1 billion bugs [Cohen

---

[*]http://smartbear.com

et al. 2006b]. They also discussed various code review strategies including the ones supported by dedicated tools, which are becoming more and more popular nowadays. But code review is just a process which involves people and relies on their knowledge. The last couple of decades was rich in literature on how to build and maintain a good design of a software system. For example, Arthur Riel describes heuristics that should be followed to achieve a good quality of object-oriented design [Riel 1996]. The "Gang of Four" summarized the most frequently used design patterns in object-oriented languages with examples in C + + and Smalltalk [Gamma et al. 1995]. Kent Beck describes the best coding practices specific for Smalltalk programming language [Beck 1997]. He also introduces a concept of *code smells* — signs of bad design practices in source code [Fowler et al. 1999]. The best programming practices may be related to a programming language or a paradigm in general, can be developed and enforced by a company for all the employees to maintain the same style or even may be based on a certain domain. Thus it is complicated to ensure maintainability, as one has to possess a significant knowledge about different best practices and ensure that a software project adheres to them.

With advances in the software engineering field, the approach of *static analysis* (also known as "automated static code analysis") [Louridas 2006] was employed to develop tools that aid developers in finding various types of issues and bugs in source code without executing it [Johnson 1978]. At the moment there are plenty of tools that check for code style, potential bugs, vulnerability issues or just suspicious constructs in source code. Such tools perform well when validated in a standalone setup. However, when it comes to the real usage during the development process static analysis support is often neglected. For example Beller *et al.* analyze large corpora of open-source projects and discover that most of them try to use static analysis, but only few succeed. The authors suggest that static analysis is really beneficial only if it is integrated into the development workflow. The same idea is advocated by the authors of InCode — an Eclipse plugin that reports code smells interactively to developers as they develop software in their IDE [Ganea et al. 2017]. Moreover, integrated static analysis reports can aid in other contexts. For example Bacchelli and Bird identified that static analysis could improve the efficiency of a modern code review [Bacchelli and Bird 2013].

During the last 30 years we saw many diverse analyzers, numerous code quality tools, and various user studies related to static analysis. As a result there are few facts and beliefs that co-exist while contradicting one another:

1. Most static analysis tools are standalone;

2. Integrated static analysis tools are more beneficial;

3. There are few IDEs and tools with integrated static analysis;

4. Most of the software evolution/comprehension research focuses on standalone tools;

5. Evaluations of integrated tools focus on a single scenario and do not consider the impact of the tools on the developers.

By summarizing all the statements presented above, we identified the following **problem:**

> *Despite the evidence of the usefulness of static analysis integrated into the development process, most of the existing development tools are not augmented with quality assistance features. Most contemporary research avoids development tools that are augmented with static analysis in favor of standalone analyzers, which are known to have deficiencies. As a result it is still unknown what is the impact of static analysis integrated into a development workflow beyond a few test subjects or a single company.*

1.1 The Assisting Ecosystem

In contrast to the related research which either evaluated a single tool or assessed performance of multiple similar tools, our goal is to change a development ecosystem to provide code quality assistance based on static analysis. Then we want to assess the feasibility of such changes in the ecosystem; the acceptance of the changes by the developers; and the impact of the changes on the development ecosystem and community.

As our **thesis** we formally state that:

Automatic quality assistance is an essential feature of software development tools that improves the development experience provided that the assistance engine supports basic adaptation to the user needs.

In this dissertation we focus on the developer community around the Pharo ecosystem[*] as well as on the changes to the ecosystem itself. We selected Pharo because it comes with a variety of development tools; it already had a standalone static analyzer included; the decision makers behind Pharo's evolution agreed to integrate static analysis feedback into the core development tools. We had a unique opportunity to observe how the developers react to the updated tools and compare the new development experience with the one that was present prior to the integration. We discovered that the live quality feedback was mostly beneficial to all the developers, changed the way they used to work, and sometimes even taught them something new. Based on the changes made to the Pharo codebase we can say that the live feedback increased awareness about the rules in the system, as some of the existing rules were replaced by the more important ones. Finally to exemplify how integrated quality assistance can aid on the various stages of a software development workflow, we integrated static analysis feedback into other tools used for debugging, inspecting, and reviewing code.

1.2 Contributions

1. *Live Static Analysis Feedback Acceptance*
   According to prior research, software developers want to receive static analysis feedback as soon as possible [Yamashita and Moonen 2013]. Moreover, the IDE's code editor is the perfect place to provide such feedback. Nonetheless only a small number of development environments provide live quality feedback, and there exists limited knowledge about the experience of developers with such tools. We integrated live quality reports into an IDE and collected user experience. Our results show that developers find this integration to be very

---

[*]http://pharo.org

useful, developers try to solve the reported issues and learn about new concepts and constraints. We discuss the findings in depth in chapter 4. Some of the results were presented previously at an international seminar [Tymchuk 2015].

2. *False False Positive Investigation*
All static analyzers suffer from false positive reports. If the ratio of these reports is high for a certain analyzer, users are reluctant to use it because the effort needed to identify false positives may be higher than the benefit of true positive reports. Naturally, researchers and analysis developers strive to decrease the false positive ratio which is often based on the user feedback of a certain analyzer. While working with the Pharo community we discovered that not all of the false positive reports provided by users are actually false positives and may mask real issues outside of the analysis domain. We discuss the example of false false positives in section 4.3. The results of this analysis were previously presented at an international seminar [Tymchuk 2017a].

3. *Impact of Quality-Aware Tools*
By augmenting an integrated development environment with static analysis feedback we made an impact on the projects that are developed using it and on the environment itself. For example we analyze the changes that happened to the quality rules themselves. After developers started to see live code critiques they were motivated to evolve the static analysis rules to increase their value. We discuss the impact in depth in section 5.2. The work previously were presented in an international workshop [Tymchuk et al. 2016a].

4. *Quality Anomalies Decomposition*
During our experiments we encountered evolution of the quality rules alongside the software evolution. Moreover, we encourage changes to the static analysis rules, as this is the only way to ensure that they fit the contemporary project requirements. However, this brings additional challenges. The historical changes of quality value are caused not only by the changes in the software system, but also by changes in the quality rules themselves. This complicates the assessment

of a software quality evolution. To deal with this issue we introduce a visual decomposition approach that reveals the abnormal quality changes caused by the evolution of rules. The visualization is described in section 5.1 and was previously presented at an international conference [Tymchuk et al. 2016c].

5. *Quality-Centric Visual Code Review Approach*
   Based on the study of the challenges in modern code review, the reviewing tools can greatly benefit from static analysis assistance. We introduced a code review approach based on a visual assessment of the system under review. The visualization is augmented with static analysis reports and thus guides code review focusing the attention of a reviewer on the parts with poor quality. The approach is described in section 6.2. The approach, together with a prototype tool were previously presented at international conferences [Tymchuk et al. 2015a;b].

6. *Unified Quality Model*
   Throughout the course of this dissertation we integrated static analysis into a few tools or implemented new tools from scratch. To reduce the engineering and maintenance efforts, we devised a unified static analysis model that reduces the cost of the quality assistance integration into a new tool. The model also simplifies integration of new analyzers. To achieve such flexibility the model is easily extendable, handles the aggregation of validation reports, and provides a convenient API for tools that want to obtain the reports and for analyzers that want to provide them. We describe the design decisions and application examples in chapter 3. The model was previously presented at an international workshop [Tymchuk et al. 2017].

Many of our engineering contributions are integrated into Pharo starting from the 5th version.* Pharo is an MIT-licensed project with a publicly available repository: `https://github.com/pharo-project/pharo`. Some of the projects that we developed are

---

*`http://pharo.org/news/pharo-5.0-released`

available separately. All of them also have the MIT license and a public repository:

QualityAssistant: a live static analysis feedback system implemented as a plugin for the main Pharo code editor Nautilus.
Artifact: [Tymchuk 2017c]
Repository: https://github.com/Uko/QualityAssistant

Renraku: a unified static analysis model for Pharo.
Artifact: [Tymchuk 2017d]
Repository: https://github.com/Uko/Renraku

ViDI: a Visual Design Inspector augmented with static analysis reports designed to perform code reviews.
Repository: https://github.com/Uko/Vidi.

1.3 Outline

This dissertation is structured as follows:

chapter 2 provides an overview of the related work with focus on the various types of static analyzers, integration of the static analysis into development tools, and studies on the static analysis usage.

chapter 3 presents the Renraku static analysis model which was shaped by the requirements of both algorithms and tools that arose during our research.

chapter 4 presents QualityAssistant — the static analysis feedback integrated into a code editor. The chapter also contains evaluation and analysis of the acceptance of QualityAssistant by software developers, and discussion about false positives.

chapter 5 describes the impact of the integration of QualityAssistant into Pharo. The chapter also presents the issues in historical quality analysis that may occur upon changes to the quality standard, and discusses how the issues can be visually resolved.

chapter 6 presents other tools that use our code quality model. Such tools include ViDI — a dedicated code review system with a built-in visualization; reimplemented Smalltalk critique browser, debugger, and a code editor.

chapter 7 concludes the thesis and discusses the future vision with possible directions for future research.

 # State of the Art

Software engineers use various practices to ensure good quality of their software. One may use software tests and benchmarks to automatically verify that a software execution produces the expected results [Dustin et al. 1999]. On the other hand, not all quality issues can be detected by testing a program execution, and it is complicated to exhaustively test all the possible execution cases especially if a software system depends on user feedback. Another approach to ensure a reasonable level of software quality is a *code review* — a practice where developers review a piece of software to detect bad practices and prevent bugs before they appear in production [Cohen et al. 2006b]. Code reviews still require significant amount of human time to analyze source code, and some of the issue detection can be automated with static analysis [Louridas 2006] by analyzing source code with software algorithms.

In this dissertation we focus on the ways to automatically provide valuable information about software quality to software developers. Most of the assistance that we can provide automatically falls into the *maintainability* sector of software quality [ISO/IEC 2010], mostly because maintainability issues cannot be easily detected by simply running a program. Some of our analyzers also recommend

accessibility improvements by analyzing UI-related actions;

interoperability warnings by detecting a usage of system-specific API;

performance efficiency solutions by pointing out inefficient implementation;

user error protection highlights by identifying potential bugs;

and much more.

We see three main categories of the research in this domain. The first category focuses on the detectors of bad practices in the source code. The second category focuses on the usage of static analysis to improve other tools, or on dedicated tools based on static analysis. The third category of related research focusses on the assessment of the usage for static analysis, its performance and shortcomings.

2.1 Static Analyzers

Table 2.1 lists some of the popular static code quality analyzers for various programming languages. Most of them check the abstract syntax tree of a software system and detect suspicious patterns that are signs of bad programming practices. Some of the analyzers focus on a compiled bytecode or a raw source code to be more efficient, or to detect issues not present in an abstract syntax tree. The Lint tool was the first of its kind, developed in 1979 to detect suspicious code in C programs. Many contemporary tools have a *Lint* suffix in their name to show the similarity with the original static analysis tool. Many studies related to static analysis focus on tools for Java, especially FindBugs. This tool can be considered to be state of the art in code quality static analysis, as it is up to date widely used by both researcher and engineering communities [Ayewah et al. 2007; Ayewah and Pugh 2010]. In this thesis we mostly use SmallLint, which shares the general principles with the other analyzers and can check textual source code, an AST, or a compiled bytecode. All the analyzers mentioned until this point fall into the *lightweight* category

Tool	Language	Reference
Lint	C	[Johnson 1978]
PyLint	Python	www.pylint.org
pyflakes	Python	pypi.python.org/pypi/pyflakes
Checkstyle	Java	checkstyle.sourceforge.net
PMD	Java	pmd.github.io
FindBugs	Java	[Ayewah and Pugh 2008]
ESLint	JavaScript	eslint.org
JSHint	JavaScript	jshint.com
RuboCop	Ruby	rubocop.readthedocs.io
Reek	Ruby	github.com/troessner/reek
Tailor	Swift	tailor.sh
SmallLint	Smalltalk	[Roberts et al. 1996]

Table 2.1: Popular static analysis code quality tools.

as they focus on the common mistakes of software developers, can efficiently validate large codebases, and are not guaranteed to detect all the defects present in the project under validation [Muske and Serebrenik 2016].

Another category of analyzers focuses on a *Code Smell* [Fowler et al. 1999] detection and mainly relies on software metrics, thresholds and fuzzy logic. IPLASMA is a pioneering tool in this category, which uses a metric-based approach to detect code smells [Marinescu 2004]. Its detection strategies capture deviations from good design principles, aggregate metrics and compare their values against absolute and relative thresholds. The DECOR methodology defines all the steps needed to specify and detect code design smells [Moha et al. 2010]. The authors of DECOR also present DETEX, a tool which implements the DECOR approach. Khomh *et al.* developed a bayesian approach which calculates the probability of an entity violating a certain design rule [Khomh et al. 2009]. The research related to *Code Smell* detection mainly focuses on the approaches to define bad code detectors either precisely, or by using statistical approaches. In comparison with lightweight analysis, these analyzers usually need more time to analyze software and the detected issues require more time to resolve. We rarely used analyzers that detect *Code Smells* in our research, as we investigate various ways to enhance interaction of a developer with static analyzers, and we could achieve a shorter feedback loop by employing lightweight analysis discussed previously.

The authors of *Usage Contracts* discuss the usability of their rule-defining Domain Specific Language (DSL) by rule developers [Lozano et al. 2015]. *Usage Contracts* operate on Smalltalk code and the rules are defined in a language similar to Smalltalk to reduce the learning barrier that the rule developers may experience when creating a *Usage Contracts* rule. The authors motivate their decisions with a previous experience with the *SOUL* [De Roover et al. 2011] language: developers were reluctant to define structural regularities in SOUL as they had to learn a new programming language. We followed this idea by having rules about Smalltalk code defined in the Smalltalk programming language. However, to our knowledge there is no dedicated study on the impact of the DSL on the productivity of static analysis rule creators.

2.2 Static Analysis Integration

According to various studies static analysis may be especially valuable when integrated into the tools that support common developer tasks. For example peer code review [Rigby and Bird 2013] is widely practiced nowadays as a part of the software development process and helps programmers to detect bugs in the early stages, and share knowledge about a code base. However, according to a recent study reviewers spend a lot of time to detect trivial issues instead of focusing on the important ones [Bacchelli and Bird 2013]. These trivial issues are usually related with the coding guidelines, and possibly can be detected automatically to save the time of reviewers. During a code review session, tools like Review Bot [Balachandran 2013] use static analysis reports to improve reviewers experience by pointing out parts that violate some rules.

The Tricorder project adds quality reports to the code review tool used by Google [Sadowski et al. 2015]. Reviewers can mark quality critiques as false positives and provide an optional textual feedback that will be sent to the quality rule developer. Usage data is collected and the Tricoder team pursues the goal to maintain the amount of false positives under 10%. Tricorder relies on 16 static analysis tools that can be applied to five programming languages. Besides having to integrate the output into their code review tool and invent a strategy to handle false positives, Google engineers had to build a sophisticated infrastructure to run all the tools on their codebase and provide a uniform result. Buckers *et al.* operated on a much smaller scale by running three static analysis tools on a single Java project and visualizing the obtained result [Buckers et al. 2017]. While the main focus of the authors is a tool that visualizes static analyses, they spend a large amount of time explaining the design decisions used to run all the analysis together and unify results. Because of the current design of static analysis tools, developers have to spend substantial amount of time to run the analysis and aggregate the reports, while their main goal is to incorporate static analysis feedback in a tool that they develop. With Renraku we propose a unified model for static analysis reports, thus a tool developer has to rely on a single API to work with static analysis.

Static code analysis tools are often embedded into Integrated Development Environments (IDEs). While using such environment a developer is informed about the quality issues in the same place that he uses to develop programs. For example, an Eclipse plugin *inCode* detects popular code smells and displays them live to a developer [Ganea et al. 2017]. The plugin also provides refactoring assistance to resolve the detected issues. The authors evaluated inCode by measuring refactoring productivity with and without the plugin. The evaluations show that the developers who use inCode can detect and resolve more violations. However, according to the state of the art, analyzers are rarely used by developers despite the positive evaluations in research papers. Thus we see the impact of the static analysis *intrusiveness* as well bundling as a default part of an IDE to be relevant and unexplored concerns.

Some IDEs provide live feedback about coding practice violations as-you-type. For example, the popular Java IDEs Eclipse and Net-Beans[*] provide simple validations of the most trivial development mistakes. IntelliJ IDEA[**] uses a custom defect detection subsystem that supports custom validations defined by user. However, there is no research that assesses the usefulness and impact of the static analyses that are integrated into these development tools.

---

[*]https://netbeans.org
[**]https://www.jetbrains.com/idea/

Static analysis can be also used during continuous integration (CI) [Duvall et al. 2007]: After the integration of a change, the software system is automatically built and validated with respect to various criteria. One of the most popular systems used for this practice is SonarQube [Campbell and Papapetrou 2013]. It defines seven axes of quality as follows: *Architecture and Design, Duplications, Coding Rules, Comments, Unit tests, Potential bugs* and *Complexity*. SonarQube lately became accompanied by an IDE plugin with live feedback called SonarLint.* The live plugin can communicate with the server counterpart and share settings. SonarSource** — the company that developed the tools — also started to introduce their own static analysis model that software developers can use to create rules for SonarQube and SonarLint. Nevertheless, SonarLint and all the related features are still in their infancy and it is hard to speculate on their future evolution.

By leveraging the user interface of development tools some developers investigated novel approaches to enhance development experience with static analysis tools. Just-in-time static analysis performs checks only on the part of source code that is being browsed or edited by a developer [Do et al. 2016]. Our QualityAssistant tool described in chapter 4 also follows the just-in-time static analysis approach because it is encouraged by the standard development tools that we extend. To help developers to solve the quality report some tools provide *quick fixes* that can automatically transform a code in question to eliminate the static analysis warning. Bari *et al.* suggest to use *slow fixes* that provide developer with additional information and functionality to aid with issue resolutions [Barik et al. 2016]. Many of our static analysis rules provide quick fixes and we also experimented with "slow fixes" in the situations when fixing could not be completely automated.

2.3 Static Analysis Usage

Although static analysis is often perceived as a helpful technology, it is rarely used in real-world projects. The creators of the Coverity static analyzer discovered many unexpected problems while trying

---

*http://www.sonarlint.org
**https://www.sonarsource.com

to commercialize their tool and bring it to software development companies [Bessey et al. 2010]. In particular the authors claim that any inconvenience such as struggling to run the static analyzer, non-understandable tool output, or even warnings with which developers disagree have a high chance to demotivate the static analysis users.

Other researchers surveyed 20 developers that used FindBugs, Lint, CheckStyle, PMD and other similar tools to investigate why software developers do not use static analysis tools to find bugs [Johnson et al. 2013]. The authors do not provide an exact answer to whether software developers use static analysis tools but rather state that "developers tend to like these tools, but there are certain reasons that stop them from using the tools". Johnson *et al.* quantitatively measure interviewees' attitudes towards the five feature groups of static analysis tools: 1) Tool Output, 2) Supporting Teamwork, 3) User Input and Customizability, 4) Result Understandability, and 5) Developer Workflows. For every group, negative feedback of the interviewees exceeded positive feedback. They find that the most impactful reasons for not using static analysis tools are the high number and a poor organization of false positives, weak support for teamwork and customizability, and poor understandability of the tool output. Also the participants of this study expressed a need to be informed about issues in their code as soon as they appear. This study summarizes the shortcomings of various static analysis tools and may miss the good features of a certain tool during the summarization. In our case, instead of focusing on the usage of many diverse static analysis tools, we augment commonly used software development tools with static analysis feedback and analyze the impact on the users.

A study of static analysis usage in open source projects discovered that many of them contain traces of static analyzers in the form of configuration files, however most of the project developers do not use static analysis on the regular basis [Beller et al. 2016]. The authors suggest that static analysis is fully beneficial only if it is integrated into the development workflow, and also they suggest to perform integration at least on the level of a CI server. While the CI server integration is already present in the Pharo development process, we take the integration to a new level by augmenting development tools with static analysis reports. As a result not only developers of a single project benefit from static analysis, but all users of the IDE.

Another survey was performed on professional software developers to identify the current status and requirements of static quality analysis [Yamashita and Moonen 2013]. The authors discovered that almost one-third of the surveyed developers did not know about the concept of code smells [Fowler et al. 1999] and anti-patterns [Brown et al. 1998]. The ones who were familiar with these concepts were mostly concerned about *Large Class*, *Long Method*, and *Accidental Complexity* [Brooks 1987]. The authors identified that developers need a user-friendly, real-time tool with customizable detection strategies that enable domain-specific detection of quality issues. Our findings confirm the importance of immediate static analysis feedback previously requested by the interviewees of this study. The authors also learned that software developers use technical blogs, programmer forums, colleagues and industry seminars as their main sources of information. Based on our findings, static analysis tools can serve alone as a source of knowledge for software developers.

Often static analysis algorithms are designed to detect Code Smells such as *God Class*, *Data Class*, *Refused Bequest*, *Feature Envy Method*, *etc*. By narrowing the scope of the code quality criteria to the generic and high level code smells described by Kent Beck [Fowler et al. 1999] researchers can easily compare various static analysis approaches or ensure applicability on various object-oriented programming languages. However, the usefulness of the generic detection strategists is questionable. According to a survey performed by Palomba *et al.*, software developers do not see a big threat in every code smell detection, and the severity of a detected smell is contextual to a software project, or even a part of a project [Palomba et al. 2014]. On the other hand, researchers showed that project-specific static analysis rules are more beneficial than the generic ones. For example violations detected by dedicated rules of a single project were addressed more often that generic violations [Renggli et al. 2010b]; domain specific rules can predict bugs more procisely [Hora et al. 2012]; more and more studies identify domain-specific rules for object-relational mapping frameworks [Chen et al. 2014], Android applications [Hecht et al. 2015], cascaded style sheets [Mazinanian et al. 2014], and the Model View Controller architectural pattern [Aniche et al. 2016]. Thus in the scope of this thesis we do not obsess with generally accepted code quality standards, but rather follow the needs of developers by providing the rules that suit their domain requirements.

Renraku

While exploring various ways of augmenting a development workflow with quality feedback we carefully chose our technology. We selected Pharo [Ducasse et al. 2017] as the main proving ground of our studies. Pharo is a rapidly evolving descendant of Smalltalk [Goldberg and Robson 1983], that was forked in 2008 from Squeak [Black et al. 2007]. As most of the canonical Smalltalk implementations, Pharo combines a dynamic object-oriented language and an Integrated Development Environment (IDE). The language comes with an advanced source code reification support which provides the basic functionality required for static analysis. The IDE part of Pharo comes with a sophisticated set of development tools that we could augment with static analysis results. The board that makes decisions about Pharo evolution was interested in refining the code quality support provided by the IDE, and agreed to integrate our artifacts into the IDE. As a result we could evaluate our approaches on real users, because almost everyone uses the same IDE to develop in Pharo. Finally, we could build our quality system on top of already existing tools, such as the SmallLint static analyzer, Refactoring Browser, Rewrite Engine [Roberts et al. 1996], the SLIME domain-specific static analysis [Renggli et al. 2010a] and others. To avoid confusion, the code examples in this dissertation will be given mostly in Smalltalk, as people familiar with this language will be able to understand the examples immediately, and the language itself can be treated as a compact pseudocode which should be understandable by a broader audience.

We have built static analysis support into various tools such as a code editor, method browser, debugger, design inspector, *etc.* Each integration requires a certain implementation effort to run static analyzers, collect the results and display them in the tool. For example, the articles about Tricorder [Sadowski et al. 2015] (a pre-commit quality feedback) and UAV [Buckers et al. 2017] (a unified static analysis visualizer) dedicate a significant space to discuss the implementation of static analysis integration. To simplify the integration process for us and give an edge to the future developers, we designed a unified model of the static analysis feedback.

On the other hand, prior research has shown that a dedicated analysis works better than a generic one [Renggli et al. 2010a]. The integration of custom analyzers is yet another issue. For example uContracts [Lozano et al. 2015] never made it to production because it was too expensive to maintain the plugin for the code editor. Some Pharo developers expressed the need to augment development tools with other kind of information, such as related issue tracker entries and test coverage information. As a result we designed our model to support extensions by other analyzers.

In this chapter we describe Renraku — the code quality model that we used throughout the course of our research [Tymchuk 2017d]. Renraku was shaped by three years of tool and analysis development, as well as user feedback. The word "Renraku" comes from Japanese (連絡) and means *communication, connection, coordination*. The main goal of Renraku is to *connect quality analyzers with development tools* and make it easy to both provide and consume an information about the quality of a software entity.

Renraku pursues two main goals to simplify:

1. the reuse of existing analyzers by various tools;

2. the integration of custom analyzers into the existing tools.

Most of the existing static analyzers such as FindBugs, Pylint, JSHint provide a limited support to define new rules and output the validation results in the plain text. Renraku is designed to be an object-oriented framework that expects that all the requirements such as defining rules, running them and processing the output are going to follow object-oriented approaches. Thus a developer will subclass a basic rule class and specialize it upon a new rule creation.

The quality reports will be actual objects as well and will have an extensible way to provide feedback or even define special behavior.

3.1 The Quality Triad

Renraku is based on three basic concepts as depicted in Figure 3.1.

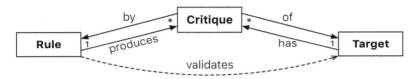

Figure 3.1: The Quality Triad of Renraku.

A **critique** is a single report about code quality. It targets a single code entity and it is based on a single quality rule. A critique is the main unit that should be used to communicate code quality information to a user. Critiques can be specialized to provide a sophisticated explanation, solution suggestions, custom tooling for problem resolution and much more. A critique does not have to be negative, it can just be a link between a rule and a target that may hold diverse information. In this case a system may contain all the possible links between all the targets and all the rules. Then a link can be re-evaluated in case the target or the rule were changed. On the other hand there might be multiple critiques connecting the same rule and target in case the target violates the rule multiple times. For example a class may have multiple unused instance variables and each critique will target a unique instance variable from the same class.

A **rule** defines a quality irregularity; it can identify an issue in a software entity and produce a critique about it. A rule can be viewed as a function that accepts an entity and returns a critique, or multiple critiques each describing a unique violation. Although a rule interacts with a target during the validation process, it does not store any direct references to the target and thus does not have any strong dependencies. Rules are also responsible for choosing a critique that is the most appropriate one for communicating an issue. For example if a visualization is needed to identify the cause of an issue the rule should use a critique capable of displaying visualizations.

A **target** is the actual piece of code that a critique targets. Potentially a target can be criticized by many critiques produced by various rules. A target should provide an interface to query its quality *i.e.,* return the critiques produced by available rules about it. The main reason for this functionality is to simplify the critique query process for potential tools. For example, when the developer of a code editor wants to add a quality feedback to his tool, obtaining the quality information should be as easy as asking the method or class itself what are its critiques. This does not have to be the only way to obtain critiques about a target, but the simplicity of the operation is important for the adoption of quality feedback in development tools.

While the Renraku triad envisions three main entities and their purpose, the system that we have built in reality is much more complicated as can be seen in Figure 3.2. In the rest of this chapter we are going to discuss the decisions taken and the pitfalls that we encountered while implementing the Renraku model.

3.2   The Critique

According to the main Renraku vision, a critique should link a quality rule to a source code target and communicate the issue discovered by the rule. In our implementation we also considered other kinds of reports not related to quality rules. Source code can have diverse sources of related data, such as code review discussions, bug reports, test coverage, or even plain text notes. All the mentioned data sources may have the same or even a higher importance than the static analysis feedback, and not every type of report is going to have some kind of a rule associated with it. We introduced `Property` — a superclass of `Critique` and other possible external properties related to a piece of source code. `Property` defines a basic interface of a title and an icon that can be used to display it in a user interface. Then `Critique` specializes `Property` by extracting the title from the rule name, selecting the icon based on a rule severity and additionally provides a description based on the rule's

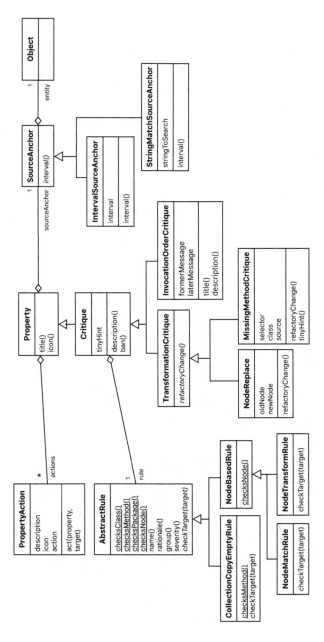

Figure 3.2: UML diagram of the main Renraku components.

```
1  relationGraphOnReverse: anObject
2      relationGraph := anObject.
3      self relationGraph build.
4      self buildReverseRoots
```

Listing 3.1: A method sends a message with a selector that no method in the system implements.

```
1  check: aMethod
2
3      aMethod messages do: [ :selector |
4        (SystemNavigation allImplementorsOf: selector)
5          ifEmpty: [ self critiqueFor: selector ] ]
```

Listing 3.2: Rule validating a method for sending messages of unimplemented methods.

rationale. Currently there are not many properties used in practice and thus in the context of this chapter we mostly focus on critiques.

3.2.1 Source Anchors

While the ideal vision of Renraku suggests that a critique points directly to a target that violates the rule, in reality our targets are source code entities that have text as their main representation. Thus a critique should also specify which code interval violates the rule. For this reason a critique points to a source anchor, which knows about the target entity and the source code interval as can be seen in Figure 3.2.

Consider Listing 3.1 which presents a method extracted from one of Smalltalk frameworks. The system has no method with the selector buildReverseRoots and thus it is highly suspicious that this method sends such a message. There are diverse approaches to identify which exact message has a selector that is not implemented by any method. One can traverse all the AST nodes, and check whether a node is a message send and whether it has a selector which does not match any method in the system. Then the rule will have a violating AST node which knows its interval in the source code. This is a good use case for a concrete source anchor that simply stores the interval itself. However AST traversal is time consuming and some AST nodes may be in the end optimized and replaced by a special bytecode. The actual rule implementation checks only the messages available directly in the bytecode as is shown in Listing 3.2. As a result the rule only knows which message violates it, but does not know the message's positions in the source code. For such cases there is a source anchor that derives the interval based on the substring location in the entitiy source code. Needless to say, the substring approach may be not precise given multiple occurrences of the same substring.

We discovered that for many critique titles it is enough to just show the name of the rule that produced the critique without significant changes. For the rest of critiques usually it is enough to add a couple of words to reasonably improve the explanation of a critique for a particular case that it addresses. For this reason we introduced a *tiny hint* property of the critique that is represented by a short string and appears at the beginning if the title before the rule's name. For example, the title of a critique about an unused variable will look like this:

[count] Instance variable neither read nor written.

In this case *count* is the variable's name, and the rest of the title is the rule's name. The tiny hint allows a developer to quickly identify the problematic piece of code while the rule's title briefly explains the issue.

3.2.2 Custom Actions

Another challenge of a good critique model design arises when rule developers need a flexible approach to provide a custom behavior to their client while staying tool-agnostic. For example a common aid provided by quality violations before Renraku was to transform the detected issue with rewrite expressions. To support this, the quality-aware tools had to check if the rule provides rewrite expressions, and execute them. Then rules of another type were introduced and they detected dependency violations. For example a common feature of many rules is to provide an automatic fix suggestion based on a source code transformation as shown in Figure 3.3.

Recently architectural critiques were introduced into Pharo, and their special feature is to open a dependency browser and point out the dependency violation. As a result all the tools had to accommodate the new critique with its new feature. Ideally we want to give rule developers the freedom to create new kinds of critiques without having to update all the tools each time. To solve this problem we introduced a concept of *PropertyAction* that has an icon and a description, as well as a "function" that accepts a property and performs the action. A property can have any number of actions, and a tool can list the actions to a programmer and execute them when needed. Figure 3.4 depicts two possible ways to display actions in the user interface. One of them lists actions as items in a context menu, another uses buttons with icons and a description popup. Whenever a menu item is selected or a button is pressed, the action will be executed.

Figure 3.5 shows the hierarchy of properties with the actions associated to them. In this case each top-level property introduces one or more actions. The note property opens a text editor to edit the note text; the issue tracker entry opens the issue in a web browser, and the critique can show a detailed description or ban* itself, if a developer decides that the report is incorrect. The subclasses of Critique inherit actions from their parent and but extend them with the ones specific to their domain. The dependency violation critique can open a dependency browser to provide additional information about dependencies and suggest a solution. The transformation critique will start a transformation process by displaying the changes that are going to take place and asking the user for approval to execute them.

3.2.3 Specializing Critiques

It is up to a rule developer to reuse available critiques to create new ones. Based on the demand of custom critiques we integrated some specialized critiques into the base distribution of the Renraku model. First of all we noticed that many critiques need a possibility to automatically resolve the issue. Thus we introduced TransformationCritique, which knows a transformation that has

---

*A critique can be banned to prevent its appearance on the same entity in the future. Usually this is done to ignore false positives.

```
visitMethodDefinition: definition
    (self methodDefinitions
        at: definition className
        ifAbsent: [
            self methodDefinitions
                at: definition className
                put: OrderedCollection new ])

    add: definition
```

```
visitMethodDefinition: definition
    (self methodDefinitions
        at: definition className
        ifAbsentPut: [
            OrderedCollection new ])

    add: definition
```

Figure 3.3: A diff suggesting a fix of a critique.

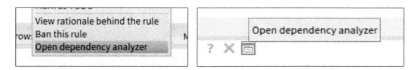

Figure 3.4: Different user interfaces display actions. On the left the actions are presented as items of a context menu, on the right — as buttons with icons.

to be applied and has an action to run the transformation. Then we added more concrete transformation critiques. For example many rules detect a missing method, and a dedicated critique can automatically construct it with a method adding transformation, and communicate which exact method is missing with a *tiny hint*.

We also noticed that a substantial number of rules detect a wrong order of messages. For example, when building a graph developers are expected to specify nodes of the graph before defining edges, and a rule may check if the nodes: message precedes the edges message. This is why we created a critique that produces an informative title based on the messages and the required order.

3.3 The Rule

The rule model of Renraku is derived from the existing design of SmallLint — the static analyzer originally available in Smalltalk [Roberts et al. 1996]. Renraku rules share the same properties as SmallLint rules: name, rationale, group, severity. The fundamental difference between SmallLint and Renraku is the ease of use. SmallLint required substantial knowledge about its implementation to use it. To validate code with SmallLint rules one had to

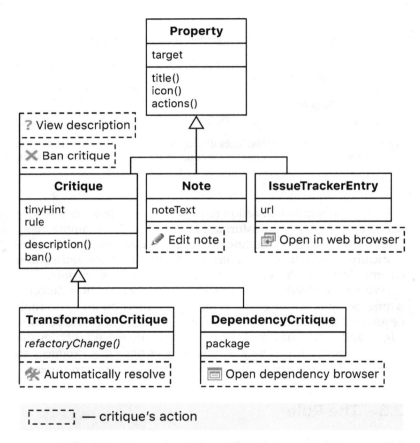

Figure 3.5: Property hierarchy with the associated actions.

```
1 | | booleanResult |
2 | rule resetResult.
3 | rule checkMethod: aMethod.
4 | booleanResult := rule critics includes: aMethod
```

Listing 3.3: Common way to run a SmallLint rule programmatically. The boolean result represents existence of a violation.

```
1 | | critiqueCollection |
2 | critiqueCollection := rule check: aMethod
```

Listing 3.4: Checking a method with a Renraku rule. The result is a collection of critique objects that describe the violations.

use dedicated checkers that had to be reconstructed or reset and queried every time, or run a rule on a source code entity and then query the rule for a result as demonstrated in Listing 3.3. Various rules had to be queried in a different way which resulted in poor quality reports integrated in tools, as the tool developers did not have time to understand how the rules should be operated. In our case, a rule can be treated as a black box that accepts a target and produces a collection of critiques about that target as demonstrated in Listing 3.4. Then a tool just has to run the rule and process the obtained critiques.

To achieve the best flexibility and performance we follow a streaming approach where a rule accepts a target to check and a callback function to evaluate for each detected critique. An example of the main checking method taken from the rule that de-

```
1 | check: aClass forCritiquesDo: aCritiqueBlock
2 |     aClass instVarNames do: [ :varName |
3 |         varName first isUppercase ifTrue: [
4 |             aCriticBlock cull:
5 |                 (self critiqueFor: aClass about: varName) ] ]
```

Listing 3.5: The main checking method of a rule that checkes classes and detects capitalized instance variables.

tects capitalized instance variables[*] is shown in Listing 3.5. The method receives a class to check, and a block to evaluate with each detected critique. Then the method iterates over all the variable names, and in case there is a variable with an initial uppercase character, the method creates a critique about this and evaluates[**] the block with the critique. This way the block will be evaluated with every critique representing a single variable violating the capitalization rule. The callback approach has a few advantages over returning a collection of critiques. When all the rules are applied to all the methods in Pharo 6 to obtain a single collection of critiques, the streaming approach provides a slight speedup of 10% because it does not create a new collection for every method-rule pair. This approach also allows a tool to run operation-heavy rules in a concurrent process and update the tool UI whenever a critique is detected. Furthermore, by using callbacks a developer can stop the rule evaluation on first encountering a critique, if she is interested only in existence of certain critiques and not the detailed report. The rule base class additionally provides convenience methods `check:`, `check:forCritiquesDo:ifNone:` and `check:ifNone:` that return a collection of the detected critiques or accept a block to evaluate if no critiques were detected.

3.3.1 Specifying a Rule Interest

Another challenge of the rule design is related to distinguishing what type of targets should be checked by a rule. For example one rule can be implemented to check methods, but will break while checking a class. SmallLint solved this by having two empty methods in the root class `checkMethod:` and `checkClass:` and rule runners will only pass a method to the first method and a class to the second one. Then the subclasses only override one of the methods depending on what they want to check. This approach gets more complicated once we have the four checking methods described previously. Additionally, during the evolution of Renraku we had to support rules

---

[*]style conventions of Smalltalk define that instance variable names should begin with a lower-case letter

[**]`value:` is the standard Smalltalk method for evaluating a block with one argument. For additional flexibility we use `cull:` in our implementation. Contrary to `value:` it will also evaluate blocks that do not expect any arguments.

for checking packages and rules for checking individual AST nodes. For this reason we introduced class-side methods[*] checksMethod, checksClass, checksPackage and checksNode. These methods return false in the base class and should be overridden to return true for rules that are designed to check one of the entity types. A rule may check multiple types of entities, for example a rule that checks if code is correctly packaged may check both methods and classes if they share the same packaging API. This approach allows rule-runners to group all the rules by the type of entity that they are checking and select the appropriate group based on the type of the entity that has to be checked.

During the evolution of Renraku our approach of declaring an interest in a target type worked well. However, when designing the *interest declaration* we envisioned a more complex scenario, when we would also have methods like checksMetaClass and checksMetaClassMethod that would by default return the value of checksClass and checksMethod respectively. The concrete rules could override the methods to specify that they want to check only the meta or non-meta entities[**]. We discovered that there is only a small number of rules that distinguish meta and non-meta entities. For rule developers it is easier to validate the meta class details during the checking phase of the rule instead of specifying a special interest with checksMetaClass and checksMetaClassMethod. As a result we have never implemented special methods for declaring an interest in meta entities. We also envisioned another strategy for declaring entity type interest that may perform better. There could be a single class method which returns an array of types the rule checks. This will not change much for classes, methods, and packages, but can simplify the rules for nodes and introduce a greater flexibility in general. Based on our experience, most of the node-based rules check for the node type in their first operation. For example many rules check something about a message or a variable. Then instead of performing a type check in the rule, developers could specify the type of an AST node they are interested in.

---

[*]In Smalltalk classes are modeled as objects *i.e.,* they have methods too. Class-side methods work similarly to static methods or other programming languages, but can be inherited and overridden.

[**]Since classes are objects too, they are instances of meta classes. Meta classes define the class-side variables and methods.

3.3.2 Specializing Rules

To collect all the rules available in the system we use the same approach used by SmallLint. We simply collect all the subclasses of the abstract rule class and then select ones that check an appropriate target type. Additionally if a certain rule wants to declare an interest in a target for all its subclasses but should not perform validation itself, it can override `isVisible` to return false for its class and exclude itself from the rules that are used to check code. By dynamically querying the subclasses we can easily add new rules to the existing arsenal if they are packaged with frameworks and libraries that a project uses.

Most of the rules subclass the base rule directly. We also introduced a few custom rules to automate repetitive tasks. One of them is an invocation order rule used to detect whether a certain message is preceded of followed by another one. All such rules traverse an AST and analyze the control flow to detect violations. We generalized the analysis into a common abstract rule and require the concrete subclasses to define only the message pair and the intended invocation order. Another large group of dedicated rules is specialized to check AST nodes. Node-based rules automatically declare interest in AST nodes and override the helper method for constructing source anchors to use the source interval provided by AST nodes. The node-checking rules include a large group of rules that work based on a pattern matching syntax. To create such a rule, a developer specifies a source code pattern that should be matched and a transformation which can be used for auto-fix. SmallLint rules based on pattern code traverse the complete AST of a method and rewrite it at the same time, then they store the rewritten version, that can be used by tools to suggest an auto-fix. The Renraku alternative checks a single node and stores the replacement node which is used to apply changes by an auto-fix critique action. This not only allows developers to check a single node, but may speed up code validation by 40%, as an AST does not have to be traversed repeatedly for each rule, but can be traversed only once while applying all the pattern code rules to every node.

3.4 The Target

The target has the fewest responsibilities to fulfill. According to Renraku any object can be a target. A rule may check a target and produce a critique about it. Targets play an important role of providing a simple API to access critiques. For example all source code related entities implement a `critiques` method that returns all critiques about this entity by all the active rules in the system. Such a method allows a tool developer to quickly obtain all the critiques about a code entity currently used in a tool. A simplified implementation of such a method is presented in Listing 3.6. The method is implemented in `Behavior`, which is a common superclass for classes and meta classes thus it knows that it has to check itself with the rules for classes. The method also includes pragma `<eProperty>` because critiques are just one type of property that can exist for this object. For this reason tools are encouraged to actually use another dedicated method `externalProperties` that collects the results from all the methods annotated with `<eProperty>` and aggregates them. The `externalProperties` method is implemented in the root of class hierarchy and thus any object can be asked for its external properties. Then analysis developers may add a method[*] with the `<eProperty>` pragma to a certain class, to make it return their properties together with the others.

3.5 Compatibility with SmallLint

SmallLint was the static analysis system of Smalltalk for many years before the creation of Renraku. As a result, many rules and tools follow the SmallLint model. To ensure a good migration from SmallLint to Renraku we maintained a healthy level of interoperatibility between the two models. SmallLint rules can be turned into Renraku rules with a help of several extension methods in the root class, while a Renraku rule can be turned into a SmallLint rule with the help of a wrapper. The main difference between them is in the checking itself and in the richness of a report. As discussed in section 3.3, a Renraku rule accepts a target to check and returns a collection

---

[*]Smalltalk allows developers to add so-called extension methods to classes of other packages.

```
1   Behavior>>critiques
2      <eProperty>
3      | rules critiques |
4      rules := ReRuleManager uniqueInstance classRules.
5      critiques := OrderedCollection new.
6
7      rules do: [ :rule |
8          rule
9              check: self
10             forCritiquesDo: [ :crit |
11                 critiques add: crit ] ]
12
13     ^ critiques
```

Listing 3.6: An implementation of a critiques method.

of critiques about it. A SmallLint rule has an internal environment where it stores the entities that violate it. When a SmallLint rule checks a code entity and detects a violation it stores the entity in the environment. Then the environment has to be queried for the inclusion of the code entity. Listing 3.7 demonstrates a Renraku checking method added to an existing SmallLint rule. First of all the method resets the rule's environment which removes all the previously detected violations. Then, depending on whether the rule checks classes or methods, the corresponding checking message will be sent with the entity as a parameter. In case a violation is detected, the resulting environment will not be empty and thus the method has to produce a critique. To declare an interest in a class or a method we can rely on the rule implementing the corresponding method (Listing 3.8). The rest of rule properties such as *name, rationale, severity, group* have the same API for both SmallLint and Renraku.

We started the migration by implementing Renraku functionality of the core SmallLint rule and then transforming the available rules one by one. The migration is going to take a long time as there are some external frameworks with SmallLint rules and we have no way to ensure that they have migrated all their rules. The migration could be automated to some extent, but each rule is unique and may store date in different formats, require resets, *etc.* Thus we

```
1   check: anEntity forCritiquesDo: aCritiqueBlock
2       self resetResult.
3       self checkClass: anEntity.
4       self checkMethod: anEntity.
5       self result isEmpty ifFalse: [
6           aCriticBlock cull:
7               (self critiqueFor: anEntity) ]
```

Listing 3.7: Renraku checking based on SmallLint functionality.

```
1   checksMethod
2       ^ self theNonMetaClass
3           includesSelector: #checkMethod:
```

Listing 3.8: Renraku type interest based on SmallLint implementation.

prefer to have Renraku functionality on top of the existing API and do a manual rule conversion, as Renraku rules may have a better implementation.

Compatibility of Renraku with SmallLint is also important because while someone may decide to convert rules to the Renraku model, certain tools (as Pharo CI server) may still expect SmallLint rules. Because SmallLint is expected to preserve a certain state, we created a wrapper that uses a Renraku rule to do the checking while pretending to be a generic SmallLint rule. Because Renraku is explicit about what it checks, the wrapper rule can easily select an appropriate environment, or check a code entity as shown in Listing 3.9. The challenge arises when a tool asks the rule's class for a uniqueIdentifierName, and the wrapper rule is a single class which instances act as diverse rules based on the rule that they wrap. Thus the wrapper rule class cannot rely on Renraku rule classes to return a correct uniqueIdentifierName. For this reason upon a new wrapper instance creation we also create an anonymous subclass that overrides uniqueIdentifierName to return the value provided by the class of the Renraku rule (Listing 3.10).

```
1  RBRenrakuWrapperLintRule>>checkClass: aClass
2
3     renrakuRule class checksClass
4        ifFalse: [ ^ self ].
5
6     renrakuRule
7        check: aClass
8        forCritiquesDo: [ :crit |
9           result addClass: aClass.
10          ^ self ]
```

Listing 3.9: SmallLint wrapper class check implementation.

```
1  RBRenrakuWrapperLintRule class>>new: aRule
2     | annotatedClass |
3
4     annotatedClass := self newAnonymousSubclass.
5     annotatedClass class compile:
6        'uniqueIdentifierName ^ ',
7        aRule class uniqueIdentifierName
       surroundedBySingleQuotes.
8
9     ^ annotatedClass basicNew
10       initialize: aRule;
11       yourself
```

Listing 3.10: SmallLint wrapper instantiation.

3.6 Creating Rules

In this section we demonstrate the common workflow to create Renraku rules. To be realistic we are going to look at an issue periodically encountered by Pharo developers. Pharo Catalog[*] is a tool for browsing and quickly installing various projects into Pharo from a dedicated repository. To add a project to Pharo catalog it is not enough to commit a configuration Class to a special repository, but one also must ensure that the configuration has project specific methods. These methods are `catalogDescription`, `catalogContactInfo`, `catalogKeywords` and they provide meta information about the project to be displayed in the catalog. Sometimes developers forget to define these methods and they cannot understand why their projects do not appear in the catalog.

We are going to develop a `ReCatalogRule` which will check if a catalog project configuration defines the required methods. The class will subclass the base `ReAbstractRule` class and override the `checksClass` class-side method to return true. Then we should also comment the class with the rule's rationale, and override the `name`, `severity` and `group` methods to specify important method properties. For this particular case we will also have a helper method `requiredMethods` that returns an array with the selectors of the required methods. The most important part of the rule is the checking method which is presented in Listing 3.11. On the lines 4 and 6 we check if the class is a configuration and if it is versioned in the catalog repository to guard ourselves against creating critiques about non-catalog classes. Then we check if there are the required methods on the class-side, and for each missing method we create a critique. At this point the rule has a basic desired functionality. The `critiqueFor:` method that we use creates basic critiques by default, which will report that a class is missing required methods but will not provide information which method is missing. For this reason we have a missing method critique that can be created by implementing a helper method presented in Listing 3.12. Then this method can be used on line 12 of Listing 3.11 to produce the critiques that will exactly specify the missing method and offer to create a stub of it. For more complicated rules a developer may want

---

[*]`http://catalog.pharo.org`

```
1  ReAbstractRule>>check: aClass
2                 forCritiquesDo: aCritiqueBlock
3
4     (self testIsConfiguration: aClass)
5        ifFalse: [ ^ self ].
6     (self testIsInCatalogRepo: aClass)
7        ifFalse: [ ^ self ].
8
9     self requiredMethods do: [ :selector |
10       (aClass theMetaClass includesSelector: selector)
11          ifFalse: [ aCritiqueBlock cull: (
12             self critiqueFor: aClass) ] ]
```

Listing 3.11: The catalog rule checking method.

```
1  ReAbstractRule>>critiqueFor: aClass missing: aSelector
2     ^ ReMissingMethodCritique
3        for: aClass
4        by: self
5        class: aClass theMetaClass
6        selector: aSelector)
7        beShouldBeImplemented
```

Listing 3.12: Missing method critique creation for the catalog rule.

to create a custom critique which can be implemented iteratively once the rule already has a working check method.

3.7 Creating Tools

As mentioned before, the convenient API to obtain critiques greatly simplifies the adoption of static analysis in tools. Designing and building a user interface is a non-trivial task that requires a substantial amount of time and various software components. To simplify the explanation we are going to exemplify the usage of critiques by using them in a software visualization. A standard demonstration of the Roassal [Bergel 2016] visualization framework often includes a script for building a polymetric visualization of a class hierarchy

```
1    b := RTMondrian new.
2    b shape box
3        height: #numberOfMethods;
4        width: #numberOfVariables.
5
6    b interaction popupView: [ :group :el |
7        group add: (RTLabel elementOn: el model name).
8        group addAll: (
9            el model critiques collect: [ :crit |
10               crit icon asRTElement ]).
11       RTHorizontalLineLayout on: group ].
12
13   b nodes: RBProgramNode withAllSubclasses.
14   b edges connectFrom: #superclass.
15   b layout tree.
16
17   b normalizer normalizeColor: [ :class |
18       class critiques size. ].
```

Listing 3.13: Roassal script to build a polymetric view for a class hierarchy.

such is the one in Figure 3.6. The visualization depicts classes as rectangles with their width mapped to the number of attributes, height — number of methods and brightness — number of lines of code. The rectangles are connected with edges that represent inheritance between classes and are laid out to form the inheritance tree. Source code for the visualization together with some features added by us can be seen in Listing 3.13.

We introduced two features into this visualization. First of all, instead of mapping the color of the rectangles to the number of lines of code, we mapped it to the number of critiques. To do this we used a color normalizer on lines 17-18 and specified that the normalization has to be based on the number of critiques[*] of each class. We also updated the popup that appears when a user hovers over an element. Now additionally to showing the name of the class,

---

[*]In this example we use `critiques` to avoid the complication that comes from the concept of external properties. In reality most of the tools including QualityAssistant use `externalProperties` to include also information of other property engines.

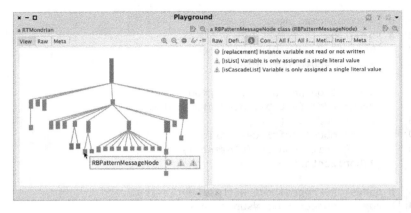

Figure 3.6: Roassal class hierarchy visualization enhanced with code critiques.

the popup also contains icons for critiques and their severity. To do this we collect all the icons of the critiques and convert them into Roassal elements, then we add all the resulting elements into the popup group on the lines 8-10. The resulting visualization can be seen on the left-hand side of Figure 3.6. By using the number of critiques to highlight the classes in red, we can easily draw attention to classes with a high number of critiques. Additionally a user may hover over a class to see its name, the exact number of critiques and their severity. The right-hand side of the figure displays an inspector on the selected object, which is in our case a class that was clicked in the visualization. This is the default behavior, as well as the critiques tab that displays the list of detected critiques. In a tool a developer may implement a similar functionality by obtaining critiques from the object and rendering their icons and descriptions, implementing interactions with them, *etc*. Our main goal is to show that using the static analysis information in tools can be easy, obtaining the number of critiques with only two messages. The tool author can inspect the properties of critiques and use them to provide even more information with a still low implementation cost.

3.8 Beyond Standard Analyzers

Renraku can support multiple backends that generate reports about external properties of a software entity. SmallLint — the default Smalltalk analyzer acted as the main and only Renraku backend during our research. This is why in the rest of the thesis we are going to focus on the static analysis critiques. In this section we describe several prototypes that showcase Renraku's potential.

3.8.1 Issue Tracker Integration

The Pharo development process includes issue tracking with Fog-Bugs.[*] To simplify interaction with the issue tracker a Ph.D. student Juraj Kubelka[**] developed an engine that analyzed FogBugs entries and linked them with the Pharo codebase. After the engine was working well, the author needed a way to display the matched issues when a developer is working with code. By registering the issue linking engine to Renraku and producing output that follows the *Property* protocol, Kubelka was able to provide the information about related issues as can be seen in Figure 3.7. The figure depicts a code editor with a method source code, and information about the issues related to this method underneath. Each list entry is related to an issue on FogBugs and briefly describes it in plain text. Then custom actions provide the user with an ability to view the details about the issue or open it in the web browser, as well as remove the issue binding or add a new related issue.

The integration with Renraku was performed in a single day and this demonstrates the ease with which an unfamiliar person can get the information from his analyzer into the development tools. The issue binding engine was never finished due a to a personal decision of its author.

3.8.2 Test Coverage

The goal of the SmartTest[***] project is to help developers to keep their code tested. The SmartTest engine creates a relation map

---

[*] https://pharo.fogbugz.com/
[**] http://www.juraj-kubelka.cz
[***] https://github.com/badetitou/SmartTest

Figure 3.7: Issue tracker entries displayed in QualityAssistant.

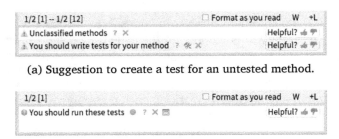

(a) Suggestion to create a test for an untested method.

(b) Warning about unexecuted tests after a change in source code.

Figure 3.8: SmartTest suggestions.

between source code and tests that are meant to validate it. When a source code entity is changed the engine may run the related tests automatically (or prompt a user) to ensure that the change did not break any of them. When a new code is created, SmartTest would suggest to create a new test for it. The code-test mapping problem is complicated because one does not want to run all the existing tests as this can take a large amount of time. If generated by the means of static analysis, test-code relations have a high chance of being not correct, because Pharo is a dynamically typed language. Performing a dynamic analysis while tests are running will slow down the execution. Besides having to resolve all the problems of test-code relations, the author has to implement a live interaction with developer as they program. With the help of the Renraku model, SmartTest live feedback was integrated into the Pharo code editor by a student in two days.

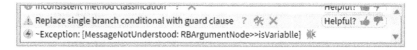

Figure 3.9: An exception property among critiques.

The top part of Figure 3.8 displays a suggestion to add a test to an untested method, while the bottom one shows a suggestion to run tests related to the method after it was changed. The author decided to add "general information" actions, as well as the actions depicted with red crosses that turn off SmartTest. The warning about a missing test has a unique action that creates a test stub. The property that notifies about unexecuted tests has two unique actions: run the related tests, and inspect the test-code bindings. The integration of test coverage information with the help of Renraku turns our attention to the fact that static analysis warnings and unit test results belong to the same category: reports about the quality of a software product.

3.8.3 Exception Properties

Renraku allows developers to easily add analyzers or even receive dedicated static analysis rules with a framework that they use. Thus there is no guarantee that at some point the code editor will not start to interrupt you with each click to report that an exception occurred in one of the analyzers that you loaded. By default we were catching all the exceptions and simply ignoring them during the evaluation/aggregation phase in Renraku. Developers who cared about the exceptions could change a setting and have all the exceptions passed down the stack and eventually debug or handle them as if they were never caught by Renraku. By exercising the flexibility of Renraku Properties we created an *Exception Property* that knows about the exception that was caught and the reified execution stack.

As can be seen on the last line in Figure 3.9 an exception property appears together with critiques. An exception entry displays the exception message and provides a debugging action that opens a debugger on the execution stack preserved in the property. This way users will not experience interruptions but will be aware that one of the analyzers rises exceptions. Developers can debug an exception in the post-mortem state to understand what caused it. This crucial feature took merely an hour to implement and did not require any changes in the existing tools. At the place where Renraku catches the exceptions a new exception property is created and added to all the other properties.

3.9 Conclusions

In this chapter we presented Renraku — an extensible static analysis model designed to conveniently connect automated software analysis and development tools. The implementation of Renraku was shaped by the requirements that we encountered during our studies. There are prototypes built to demonstrate the flexibility of the framework in combination with various tools. The tools that use Renraku are described in chapter 6. There are also prototypes demonstrating non-rule-based critiques (also known as external properties) and their compatibility with the existing tools. Finally, the live static analysis feedback based on Renraku and provided by QualityAssistant was used by *ca.* 500 developers during three years.

For the analysis developers Renraku provides an easy way to plug in their analyzer into the system. The main requirement that the developers have to satisfy is to provide the results of their analysis in the form of external properties defined by Renraku. The analysis developers are free to define the title and the icon of their properties as well as multiple actions — the entities with a description, an icon and a function that will be performed upon the action's activation. By default the external properties will use a source anchor that points to an entity targeted by an external property (such as a class or a method), but the developers can also use custom source anchors to point to a specific code interval.

Renraku provides a dedicated class hierarchies of rules and critiques for the SmallLint-style static analysis. A developer can easily create a rule by defining the basic properties such as the name, the rationale, and which type of entities can be validated by the rule. The developer should also implement a basic checking algorithm that accepts an entity to validate, checks it and evaluates the callback with a default trivial critique. Afterwards a developer may update the algorithm to produce more sophisticated critiques that have better ways to explain the detected issues and provide actions to resolve them. Renraku also comes with specialized rules that simplify common tasks such as a code rewriting based on patterns, or a validation of an invocation sequence.

For the tool developers Renraku provides a simple interface to obtain external properties about an entity based on the currently registered analyzers. The tool developer can also use the API based on callbacks to progressively obtain properties as the analyzers report them and not wait for the complete batch. The tool developers do not need to possess a detailed knowledge about the analyzers, but should rather make use of the high-level API to display the information and provide interaction with properties and their actions. This is how the domain-specific implementation is shifted from the tool developers to the analysis developers.

We believe that Renraku still has a long way to go and many challenges to face. While the concept of a single static analysis model worked for several diverse prototypes, it may include shortcomings that can be revealed only when tested by a reasonable number of real users. At the moment Pharo developers just start to express interest in Renraku and use it for simple tasks. We expect that in the near future Renraku will be applied to more complicated scenarios that will reveal its shortcomings and may motivate further evolution. However, these questions are outside of the scope of this dissertation.

QualityAssistant. Design & Reception

Designing a good tool is a complicated task, and tools that detect software defects are not an exception. Furthermore, even useful tools are often not used by software developers [Johnson et al. 2013]. Researchers who study the usage of static analysis, suggest to have the analysis tools integrated into a development workflow, and even provide evidence that developers wish to have a live code quality feedback [Yamashita and Moonen 2013]. The default Pharo distribution already included a standalone static analysis tool which was not commonly used. Thus we took inspiration from inCode [Ganea et al. 2017] and the live code quality feedback of IntelliJ IDEA, and decided to augment the main code editor of Pharo with a live and intrusive static analysis feedback. Our goal is not only to provide Pharo developers with useful information, but also to understand how they react to the new intrusive feature, and what is the impact of the intrusive reports, especially considering the previous availability of the on-demand static analyzer in Pharo.

The project started as a standalone plugin called QualityAssistant in the spring of 2015. Half a year after that QualityAssistant was integrated into the development version of Pharo 5, which was released to the public in the spring of 2016. We are going to mostly focus on QualityAssistant after it was integrated into Pharo. We do not think of QualityAssistant as a plugin, but rather view it as a strategy for maintaining live static analysis validation and as a simplistic extension of the IDE's User Interface (UI) to display the reports. Together with the main QualityAssistant functionality we shipped plugins for the Inspector and Spotter tools. These plugins never attracted a reasonable amount of users because of the nature of the tools, but they may still find their use cases in the future. We describe the plugins in more details in Appendix B.

For the static analysis algorithms QualityAssistant uses SmallLint rules [Roberts et al. 1996]. As a result, quality rules are implemented in plain Smalltalk code and can be packaged and distributed as any other project. A subset of SmallLint rules is also used by the Pharo development CI server and the complete rule base is employed by CriticBrowser (section 4.1) — the on-demand static analysis tool that is shipped with Pharo for many years. The rule base consists of about 135 rules grouped into 12 categories. Some of the larger categories are related to bugs, optimizations, style or design flaws, while the smaller categories contain rules related to a specific project or API evolution. Each rule can have one of three severity levels: information, warning and error. In general the rules are comparable to those of FindBugs, CheckStyle or PMD — the tools often used in related research. Despite the focus on SmallLint rules in this chapter, QualityAssistant can display other external properties because it operates on the Renraku model which we explained in chapter 3. In fact, QualityAssistant is the main user of Renraku, and played an important role in the migration of SmallLint rules to the Renraku model. In this dissertation we still refer to them as "SmallLint rules" to emphasize that these are conceptually the same rules that came from the previous Smalltalks and were used in Pharo before the arrival of QualityAssistant.

The user interface of QualityAssistant resides in the main code editor of the Pharo IDE. The editor is based on the Smalltalk *system browser* design and so displays code about only one class or method at a time [Goldberg and Robson 1983, Chapter 17]. Figure 4.1 displays the code area section of Pharo's code editor. At the bottom of the code editor, QualityAssistant displays a small list of quality violations that are present in the active entity such as package, class, method, *etc.* The violations are recomputed each time an entity is selected, saved or even updated by the means outside of the editor. This way QualityAssistant ensures that a user sees the most up to date information about the critiques.

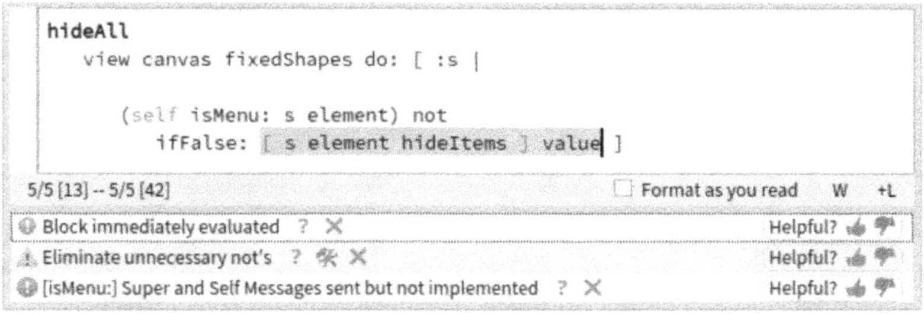

```
hideAll
    view canvas fixedShapes do: [ :s |

        (self isMenu: s element) not
            ifFalse: [ s element hideItems ] value ]
```

5/5 [13] -- 5/5 [42]	☐ Format as you read W +L
ⓘ Block immediately evaluated ? ✕	Helpful? 👍 👎
⚠ Eliminate unnecessary not's ? ✂ ✕	Helpful? 👍 👎
ⓘ [isMenu:] Super and Self Messages sent but not implemented ? ✕	Helpful? 👍 👎

Figure 4.1: Code area of Pharo's code editor with QualityAssistant in the lower part.

Each list entry refers to one issue detected by a quality rule. Clicking on an entry highlights the relevant part in code. A list entry starts with an icon that symbolizes the severity of the issue based on the corresponding property of the SmallLint rule. The severity icon is followed by a short description of an issue that may be prefixed by a tiny text hint surrounded by square brackets. For example the critique of isMenu: in the last line in Figure 4.1 hints which message is not implemented. The short description is followed by actions that can be defined by the critiques themselves. Three common actions for all the rules are: *view rationale, ban critique,* and *apply auto-fix.* When viewing the rationale of a rule a developer is presented with a longer and more detailed description of the quality violation. By banning a critique, developers can avoid the critiques of the same rule from appearing again in the scope of the method where a critique is banned, or its class or its package. Finally, some rules provide a possibility to automatically resolve the issue. The auto-fix can be any code transformation implemented as a composite refactory change [Roberts 1999]. Before an auto-fix is applied, the developer is presented with the proposed changes in the form of a unified diff as shown in Figure 4.2.

For each critique a user can press *thumbs up* or *thumbs down* buttons situated on the right side of the list. By doing this she can send us a feedback of whether the critique was helpful to her or not. Optionally a textual description can be also provided with the feedback. By collecting this data we are able to quickly identify

49

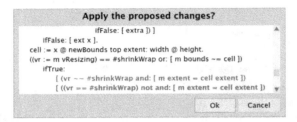

Figure 4.2: A dialog proposing changes that can fix a critique.

issues in the quality rules and detect which rules are not welcomed by the developers.

One of the main goals of the QualityAssistant assessment is to understand how live static analysis feedback compares to an on-demand tool. Thus QualityAssistant mainly runs the same rules that were present in the system and used by CriticBrowser (the on-demand tool), but displays them immediately while a developer works with a piece of software.

We believe that the concept of QualityAssistant is not bound to Pharo and may be replicated for other languages and IDEs. However, there are certain features of Pharo that simplified the implementation of QualityAssistant. Based on our experience we identified three major problems that one may encounter while integrating a live static analysis feedback into a development environment.

Scoping. Live feedback has to be related only to the small scope developer is working on *e.g.,* a single method. When applied to a larger scope, the computation will take more time and a developer will have to process more information that is not related to what she is doing. In the Pharo code editor a developer can browse only a single class or method definition at a time and we used the currently browsed entity as the scope of our live analysis.

Responsiveness. Static analysis takes time to compute. As mentioned before reducing the scope significantly reduces the duration of computation, but this often is not enough to provide a live experience. Consider performing asynchronous computation with update callbacks for detected violations. In

Pharo each class and method is recompiled upon modification, thus the complete system is always compiled. As a result we could always query the bytecode of any method in case a rule required that data.

Feedback Loop. After the integration of QualityAssistant into Pharo, developers started to encounter bugs in the static analysis rules that were present in the system for several years. While developers could simply ignore the rule by not applying it in the prior on-demand tool or not using the tool at all, we had to assist in bug fixing a few weeks after the QualityAssistant integration. The well established communication in the Pharo community allowed the developers to easily reach us and inform about the issues that they encountered.

Some of the scoping and responsiveness solutions were described previously by related research for the Android framework [Do et al. 2016]. The authors applied their static analysis on the piece of code currently focused in the scroll pane of the code editor, and dynamically displayed the detected violations, while the analyzer was running in the background.

In this chapter we assess QualityAssistant from the human perspective. In section 4.1 we provide the detailed information about CriticBrowser — the standalone static analysis tool originally available in Pharo long before the QualityAssistant integration. In section 4.2 we present the first survey about the QualityAssistant usefulness conducted a few months after its integration into a development version of Pharo. section 4.3 discusses the challenges and pitfalls of a correct false positive reports identification. Finally, in section 4.4 we analyze in details the positive acceptance of QualityAssistant based on interviews conducted with software developers.

4.1 The Precursor: CriticBrowser

Originally the SmallLint static analyzer was a part of the Refactoring Browser [Roberts et al. 1996] that was eventually integrated into VisualWorks Smalltalk [ParcPlace98 1998]. In 2002 the Refactoring

Browser together with SmallLint was ported to an open source[*] Smalltalk implementation called Squeak [Black et al. 2007]. Pharo was forked from Squeak in 2008 and inherited SmallLint together with Refactoring Browser. In 2012 Pharo 2.0 was released with a dedicated SmallLint UI called CriticBrowser. Although we often say that we compare QualityAssistant with CriticBrowser, in reality we investigate the impact caused by the integration of a live intrusive quality feedback into an IDE that had an on-demand static analyzer built in and available to developers for many years.

It is worth mentioning that the developers of CriticBrowser confused the word *critique* (an instance of criticism) with *critic* (a person who criticizes). Thus the name of the tool is CriticBrowser and all the occurrences of *critiques* were called *critics*. During our work on QualityAssistant we mostly replaced the usage of *critic* with *critique*, but kept the title of the tool unchanged.

CriticBrowser is a graphical tool that allows a developer to select a subset of SmallLint quality rules that will be used to analyze a selected list of software packages. The result of this analysis is presented in a window on Figure 4.3. The top half of the CriticBrowser window consists of a tree list of quality rules on the left and the list of violating entities on the right. The bottom half of the window is dedicated to the source code of a selected entity of the rationale of a selected rule. A small row of buttons in the middle allows a developer to change the rules and packages that CriticBrowser operates on, mark a critique as a false positive (technically known as *banning*), apply the auto-fix if a critique is produced by a transformation rule, or browse a criticized code entity in a coding browser.

In the **quality rules** pane the rules are grouped into categories and presented as a tree list. When a rule is selected, all the critiques produced by these rules are displayed in the critiques pane. At the same time the rule's rationale is displayed in the source code pane.

The **critiques** pane contains a list of classes and methods that violate the selected rule. Selecting one of them will show its source code, and allow a developer to ban the critique from appearing in the future. Certain rules allow automated resolution of the critique by source code rewriting.

---

[*]Originally Squeak was released under a Squeak license, then relicensed to Apple Public Source License, then Apache License, and now it is licensed with MIT.

Figure 4.3: CriticBrowser panes: ① quality rules; ② a rule's critiques; ③ criticized source code.

The **source code** pane displays the source code of a selected entity and highlights a section detected by the quality rule. A developer can modify the code in place and save it. For the rules that allow an automatic resolution, the code area displays a unified diff of proposed changes.

4.1.1 CriticBrowser Survey

To understand how Pharo developers work with static analysis we conducted a survey while CriticBrowser was the only static analysis tool available in Pharo. In total 46 developers participated in the survey. We asked them to identify their programming experience in years both exclusively for Pharo and for Smalltalk in general. The survey participants could also provide the source of their experience as academia or industry (not exclusively). The summary of the participant experience is shown in Figure 4.4. Most of the participant experience in Pharo is normally distributed on a range from zero to seven years. Also the participants have a diverse experience in Smalltalk development, with a large group of them developing in Smalltalk for more than ten years. The number of participants from

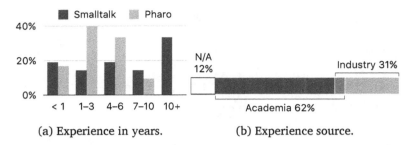

(a) Experience in years.   (b) Experience source.

Figure 4.4: Development experience of CriticBrowser survey participants.

academia is almost twice as high as the number of participants from industry.

In this survey we wanted to obtain the answers for the following questions:

RQ1 How often do developers use CriticBrowser?

RQ2 How often do developers automatically resolve critiques?

RQ3 How often do developers mark a critique as a false positive because the critique is not important?

RQ4 How often do developers mark a critique as a false positive because they do not have time to resolve it at the moment?

First of all, we asked the developers whether they know about the CriticBrowser tool. *Nine percent* of the participants specified that they do not know about the existence of the tool. Then we asked the remaining participants how often they use CriticBrowser based on a 5-point Likert [Oppenheim 2000] scale: 1. daily, 2. weekly, 3. monthly, 4. yearly, or 5. never. The obtained responses, including the participants who are not familiar with CriticBrowser are shown in Figure 4.5. Only a quarter of the survey participants use CriticBrowser on a daily basis. Another quarter uses it weekly. Usually software systems evolve rapidly and change every day. For example, the development cycle of Pharo 5 lasted for 13 months during which about 680 incremental patches were made. On average there were around 12 patches released each week and each patch contains a solution to at least one issue tracker entry, but usually there are two

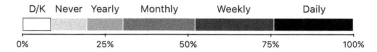

Figure 4.5: CriticBrowser usage. *D/K* — Did not know about CriticBrowser.

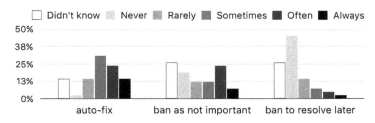

Figure 4.6: Usage of CriticBrowser features.

or three of them. Needless to say, if a developer runs static analysis on such a system only once a week, he has to process all the critiques brought by 12 patches which were ignored during the week and could cause program failures. Half of the survey participants use CriticBrowser rarer than on the weekly basis, do not use it at all, or even do not know about it. In our opinion, this indicates that CriticBrowser is not really used by most developers.

To answer the rest of the research questions, we asked the developers whether they know about the auto-fix and critique ban features. Then we asked how often they use the feature (in certain context in case of banning) on a 5-point Likert scale: 1. never, 2. rarely, 3. sometimes, 4. often, or 5. always. The responses are shown as a bar chart in Figure 4.6. The usage frequencies are situated on the X axis grouped by feature and the percentage of responses is represented on the Y axis. About 15% of the participants that know about CriticBrowser are not aware about its auto-fix capabilities and 25% are not aware about the banning feature. Those who know about auto-fixes are normally distributed. When it comes to critique banning, about 25% of developers ban critiques when they do not seem to be important. Banning of the critiques because of the lack of time to resolve them is not a common practice among the participants of our survey.

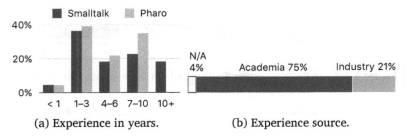

(a) Experience in years. (b) Experience source.

Figure 4.7: Development experience of QualityAssistant survey participants.

4.2   QualityAssistant Usability Survey

Almost two months after QualityAssistant was integrated into the development version of Pharo, we conducted a survey to understand how developers are using it. The survey had similar structure to the CriticBrowser survey described in subsection 4.1.1. This time 29 developers participated in the survey. Five participants did not know about QualityAssistant, which is most likely because they did not use the latest development version of Pharo at that time. As we want to evaluate the usefulness of QualityAssistant in the rest of the survey we consider only the responses of the 24 developers who are familiar with the live feedback in Pharo. Their development experience summary is shown in Figure 4.7. In this survey most of the participants have from one to three years of development experience both in Pharo and Smalltalk. Also there are almost no participants with less than one year of experience. The participants from academia make up three quarters of the whole surveyed sample.

In the CriticBrowser survey we asked developers how often they use the CriticBrowser. QualityAssistant is integrated in the development main coding browser and developers involuntarily use it all the time when they develop. Thus we found it more appropriate to assess whether developers find QualityAssistant useful or distracting. We asked the survey participants to grade the main coding browser live quality feedback on a 7-point Likert scale: 1. very useful, 2. useful, 3. sometimes useful, 4. not influential, 5. sometimes disturbing, 6. disturbing, or 7. very disturbing. The responses of the

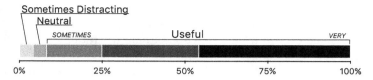

Figure 4.8: Usefulness of QualityAssistant in the code editor.

survey participants are summarized in Figure 4.8. Such a result is surprisingly positive, as the developers' IDE changed in an intrusive way, and around 90% of our respondents find it useful to some extent. Moreover, 50% of the developers find it *very useful*.

4.2.1 Feature Usage

To understand in better detail how developers are using QualityAssistant we identified 6 major features of the coding browser extension:

1. Display the description of a rule;

2. Highlight the part of the code that a critique refers to;

3. View the diff of a proposed automated critique resolution;

4. Apply an automated critique resolution;

5. Ban a critique for the entity it refers to;

6. Ban a critique for a broader scope.

Initially we asked participants whether they are familiar with each feature. In case they were familiar we asked them to specify how often they were using a feature out of 5-point Likert scale: 1. always, 2. often, 3. sometimes, 4. rarely, or 5. never. If the participants did not know about a feature we asked them whether they plan to use it. As can be seen in Figure 4.9, many participants do not know about QualityAssistant's features. For the features 1–4 all the "not knowing" developers expressed an unanimous enthusiasm to try out the features in the future.

Detailed description dialog is the best known feature and most of the developers are casually using it while none of them specified the *never* and *always* options. We find this to be natural, because once developers see a critique from a new rule they want to learn the rationale behind it, but they do not read the rationale over and over again every time they see the same critique.

Almost 40% of the participants did not know that they can **highlight** the faulty code interval by clicking on a list entry. Those who knew about the feature were using it regularly. At the time of the survey highlighting was the only way to see which interval in the source code violates a rule.[*] Thus we saw the high number of participants not knowing about this feature as a serious issue.

When it comes to the **auto-fix** functionality the feedback regarding developers not knowing about the features is confusing. To apply an auto-fix one has to go through the diff dialog, but more developers stated that they do not know about the diff dialog in comparison to the ones that do not know about the auto-fix feature. We suppose that some survey participants were confused about the diff preview question because they consider the diff dialog to be an inseparable part of the auto-fixing feature and assumed that they do not know about another special diff view. Originally we distinguished diff viewing and auto-fix application to understand if developers view an auto-fix suggestion but do not apply it. Based on the obtained responses we can say that the usage distribution is similar for the two features which means that most of the auto-fix suggestions are commonly accepted. It is worth noticing that the auto-fix usage has the same distribution in the CriticBrowser survey which suggests that the liveness of the quality feedback does not affect the developer preferences on applying automated critique resolutions.

Finally, when it comes to the **banning features**, not only did many developers not know about them, but also these are the only features that some developers do not plan to use. Out of the "not knowing" developers around 15% and 40% did not plan to use the banning and the scoped banning features respectively. The restraint towards banning was already visible during the CriticBrowser survey. In case of a simple ban in QualityAssistant the majority of developers rarely use it in contrast to the CriticBrowser results where the majority does not use the banning feature at all. We be-

---

[*]Renraku's tiny hints and inlined code editor critiques were added later.

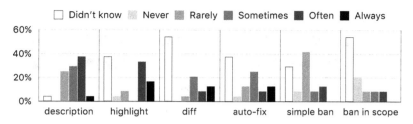

Figure 4.9: Usage of QualityAssistant features.

lieve that this is caused by the intrusiveness of QualityAssistant. In the case of CriticBrowser developers could choose just not to use it. We supposed that the possibility to ban critiques on a broader scope will be well-received, but according to the survey results developers do not care about it. We suppose that this is caused by the poor scoping possibilities of this feature at the time when we performed the survey. At the release time, QualityAssistant could ban method critiques on a class level to ensure that the critique is not going to appear on any method of the class any more. Most developers did not have use cases to perform such actions in the two month that they worked with QualityAssistant. Some time after the survey we received requests to extend the scope of banning to packages and the whole Smalltalk image.

4.2.2 Reaction to Rule Changes

The integration of QualityAssistant into the development version of Pharo motivated a couple of changes in the Pharo rule base prior to the survey. First of all the *"Probably missing yourself"* rule which we describe in details in Appendix A was completely removed. The rule checked whether a certain method is called in the end of a method cascade, because in some cases the absence of the method could manifest in a bug. In reality however, this rule was generating many false positive critiques and was distracting developers more than aiding them. With the introduction of QualityAssistant developers started to see the false positives more often and thus the rule was removed. At the same time, one of the core developers acknowledged the power of the live critiques and added a new rule that informed developers about the recent API changes. The rule

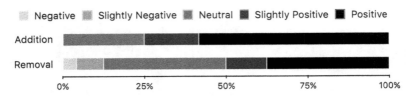

Figure 4.10: Reaction to the changes in rules. Top: addition of the *"use ifNotEmpty: method instead of ifNotEmptyDo:"* rule; Bottom: removal of the *"missing yourself"* rule.

suggested developers to use `ifNotEmpty:` and `ifNotNil:` methods instead of `ifNotEmptyDo:` and `ifNotNilDo:` respectively. The methods `ifNotEmptyDo:` and `ifNotNilDo:` should not be used by developers, but are not deprecated because many core projects still rely them and the deprecation messages would cause inconvenience.

The changes of the rule base indicate that the live feedback of QualityAssistant catalyzes the adaptation of the rules to the developer needs by constantly showing critiques of currently available rules. However, we did not know whether the majority of the developers supports the changes. To answer this question we asked the survey participants to rate both addition of the new rule and removal of the old one on the 5-point Likert scale: 1. positive, 2. slightly positive, 3. neutral, 4. slightly negative, or 5. negative. As can be seen in Figure 4.10, developers are mostly positive about the changes made to the SmallLint rules. The number of neutral impressions was also considerably high, but this can be caused by the developers not having enough time to experience the change before we conducted the survey. Three quarters of the participants found the addition of the new rule to be positive, while the rest were neutral about it. When it comes to a removal of the rule, only half of developers found it positive, and almost 10% found it negative. Maybe the negative tint is caused by the human nature that makes it hard to let things go, but this case was especially surprising to us. As mentioned before, the removed rule was detecting a very high number of false positives and we expected more positive reaction to its removal. By investigating this and other use cases we discovered that some of the false positive reports detected by developers are false false positives and we address them in more detail in section 4.3.

4.2.3 Survey Summary

The first QualityAssistant survey was an important milestone in our journey towards quality-aware tooling. We assessed whether the quality feedback that we integrated into development tools is useful for developers. The static analysis integration into the Nautilus coding browser was perceived as useful to some extent by 90% of the survey participants. This gave us confidence to continue evolving the live feedback in QualityAssistant and opened new questions such as why the acceptance is so positive. On the other hand, the Inspector and Spotter extensions were not as popular, which is not surprising as developers do not use these tools to write code. After seeing the interview results we decided not to invest much time into the Inspector and Spotter extensions unless we could completely rethink how they should be used.

We discovered that many developers still do not know about most of the QualityAssistant features. We decided to focus especially on the highlighting feature, because there is evidence of its usefulness but almost 40% of developers do not know about the feature. The auto-fix and banning features did not seem to have a big difference from the usage in CriticBrowser. We understood that we need to pay more attention to the scoped banning feature, as it was not used as much as we expected it to be.

Finally we had our first glimpse on the changes to the rules caused be the QualityAssistant integration. The developers found the changes to be mostly positive which motivated us to analyze all the changes that happened to rules in Pharo 5. Additionally, we saw that some developers were skeptical about a rule removal which we expected to be absolutely positive. Thus we decided to investigate in more detail what developers think about the critiques produced by various rules and how does this align with false positives.

4.3 False False Positives

Integration of QualityAssistant into the main Pharo code editor made developers more aware about quality rules available in Pharo, as they began to see critiques about their code involuntarily. Needless to say, none of the developers wanted to be distracted by a critique which was faultily identified. As a result we experienced multiple rule fixes, rants about false positives, and rule removal proposals or even rule removals motivated by a high number of false positives. In this section we share our experience of dealing with false positives and false false positives (FFPs), as some of the false positive reports identified by the developers turned out to be true.

4.3.1 The False False Positive Concept

Static analysis tools may produce incorrect detections (false positives), which negatively impact the overall usability of these tools. Usually this happens because of the lack of information present in the source code. In case of a high false positive ratio, a developer who inspects static analysis results may spend significant amount of time trying to address the incorrect detections. Thus, a high number of false positives can decrease the overall usefulness of a static analysis tool.

As false positives are a critical issue for static analysis users, there is constantly an effort to mitigate them. Bessey *et al.* suggest to keep the ratio of false positives under 20-30% to make a tool acceptable by users [Bessey et al. 2010]. Google went even further and built their static analysis environment in a way that it automatically suppresses every rule that has more than 10% of false positive reports based on the user feedback [Sadowski et al. 2015]. However, the definition for false positives in static analysis quite often diverges from the common sense. According to the Merriam-Webster dictionary[*] a false positive is *"a result that shows something is present when it really is not"*. On the other hand, some users of static analysis classify reports as false positives if they do not understand the rationale behind the reports, or simply do not think that the reports are important for them [Bessey et al. 2010]. No one can forbid people to express their opinion that true positives are false, and such cases should not be ignored. But we believe that the community around static analysis should not confuse the false positives identified by users with the real ones. First of all this will distort the false positive ratio and secondly this will mask real issues, such as poor understandability of a report. The reality is quite the opposite, for example researchers from Google state that for their study "developers will decide what a false positive is" [Sadowski et al. 2015]. In other words: when a

---

[*]https://www.merriam-webster.com/dictionary/false%20positive

person sick with tuberculosis says that his tuberculosis test is false positive, this neither cures the tuberculosis, nor does it make the test incorrect. But if a software developer identifies a static analysis report as a false positive, then the anti-patterns in her code are not anti-patterns any more, and the false positive ratio of the detection rule suddenly increases.

We believe that the poor acceptance of static analysis reports is partially caused by the naming used in such tools. For example a developer starts to use a tool called FindBugs, and she expects that (as the name suggests) the tool will find bugs. Then the tool detects a bad practice, for example that a class has no comment. But the project still works despite the detection. The developer makes a conclusion that this is not a bug and thus the report has to be a false positive. Originally static analysis was deployed as a part of the development process with a strictly specified workflow that consisted of running static analysis on the whole system, triaging the reports to identify false positives, and resolution of the true positive results. This workflow was described by Flash Sheridan a few years ago while discussing the benefits and challenges of static analysis deployment in software companies [Sheridan 2012]. Sheridan also mentions FFPs — correct violations falsely discarded by novice programmers which may cause a loss of important information. From this perspective, incorrectly identified false positives appear as a threat for companies who use static analysis, while at the same time they are responsible for the incorrect identification.

When we consider such tools as QualityAssistant, they work more as assistants (or pair programmers) pointing out suspicions things in source code, but not forcing you to change them. One of QualityAssistant's rules detects whether there is a temporary variable that is declared, but never read nor written. The rule cannot produce false results, as all the information about temporary variables is available in method definitions. We believe that in a similar manner a pair programmer would point out the fact that a temporary variable is declared but never used. We are also aware of developers who do not like to see the information about unused variables. For example, a developer may want to suppress information about unused variables in a piece of code under development, because she has not written statements that use newly defined variables yet. Although a developer can identify the reports described in this example as false positives, the static analysis community has to focus on the problem with the tool output or its timing, and not with false positives. The rule that detects unused variables cannot be improved in any way, because it already detects them with the maximum precision. However, we believe that the development tool can be updated to present the information in a different time period or in another way which will be more acceptable by the developer. In this section we exemplify various FFPs and describe how they are caused by tool deficiencies, misunderstanding, or an ignorance towards certain groups of developers.

4.3.2 The True False Positives

First of all, we want to specify what we treat as the true false positives. As a false positive of a critique we identify a rule violation report that does not conform to the rationale of the rule. For example there was a new rule introduced into Pharo which suggested to assert test results with

```
self assert: value equals: expected
```

instead of

```
self assert: (value = expected)
```

The former expression provides a more descriptive output. However, the `assert:` method is defined on the top level of the class hierarchy and it is a common practice to make assertions in your code to express contracts (*i.e.,* preconditions, invariants and postconditions). For example one can have the following assertion in an algorithm:

```
self assert: (aCollection size = 1)
```

The rule also detected assertions outside of the test classes and such critiques were false positives as the `assert:equals:` method is defined only for tests and cannot be applied outside of the testing framework. This false positive is caused by a bug in the detection rule. The rule can easily check if the assertion is performed in a test class and eliminate previously discussed false positives.

Another more classic example of a true false positive is caused by a lack of information. One useful newly introduced rule detects issues related to the use of the Roassal [Bergel 2016] framework. When building a graph with this framework you are expected to specify nodes of the graph before defining edges. Thus the rule checks if an `edges` message is preceded by a `nodes:` message. However Pharo is dynamically typed and the rule has no way to make sure that the receiver of the checked messages is a graph builder. This ambiguity will result in false positives as soon as there is another interface with `nodes:` and `edges` methods. This issue cannot be solved easily, but there are strategies that the rule may follow, to reduce the false positive ratio. For example the detection algorithm can use type inference [Palsberg and Schwartzbach 1991] or dynamic analysis [Ball 1999] to obtain the type of the messages receiver. Alternatively the rule can detect only the cases where a instance of the graph builder is created and immediately initialized. This will greatly lower the recall of this rule because it will miss all the cases where the graph builder is passed as an argument to a method or returned by another object. On the other hand, such a change will increase the precision, as the rule will be sure about the type.

In both cases false positives were caused by the issues in the algorithm. They can be simple bugs or more complicated limitations of the environment where the algorithm is executed. In case of the true false positives it is the responsibility of the rule designer to act in that situation.

4.3.3 The False False Positives

While analyzing developers' preferences about quality rules, we discovered that there are rules that are not favored by some developers although they detect exactly what they intend to. Some of these rules are general best practices like a warning about a declared but unused variable, uncommented class, or a debugging statement left in source code. All these critiques are indeed bad practices which should not be present in the final version of an application and will not be integrated in the Pharo code base. However, some developers do not want to be bothered with such critiques while they develop, and would rather focus on them when they are about to commit the final version. This suggests that such rules should be applied in a pre-commit phase and not continuously while a developer is

```
1    background ifNil: [ ^ true ].
2
3    (background isColor and: [
4     background isTranslucentButNotTransparent ])
5        ifTrue: [ ^ true ].
6
7    (border isColor and: [
8     border isTranslucentButNotTransparent ])
9        ifTrue: [ ^ true ].
10
11   ^ false
```

Listing 4.1: The "quick return" approach.

programming. This reasoning can be done only if we acknowledge that there is an issue which is not a false positive, because it cannot be solved by updating the rule, but can only be solved by rethinking the static analysis tooling.

One more complicated rule was checking if there are multiple if-statements that returned a boolean literal from a method and suggested to replace them with a compound conditional expression. For example in Listing 4.1 the conditional expressions on the first nine lines check if some conditions are met and then return true from the method. In case the execution does not trigger the conditional expressions, the rest of the method is executed *i.e.,* false is returned.

The rule suggests to use the implementation demonstrated in Listing 4.2. This way all the conditions are incorporated into a single compound boolean expression. According to one of the developers this is a bad rule as it is less readable. A more detailed mailing list discussion revealed that most developers also find the implementation in Listing 4.1 easier to comprehend than the one in Listing 4.2. Moreover, no one from the Pharo community knows who implemented the rule, and many developers suggest to remove it completely. The rule cannot be improved in any way, as this is not a false positive, although it does not help developers. Blind removal of the rule based on the developer requests will eliminate its useless critiques, but will not answer the question of why the rule was created. We believe that in this case the community has to

```
1  ^ background isNil or: [
2
3     (background isColor and: [
4        background isTranslucentButNotTransparent ]) or: [
5
6     border isColor and: [
7        border isTranslucentButNotTransparent ] ] ]
```

Listing 4.2: The compound boolean logic.

```
1  (denominator = 0)
2      ifTrue:  [ Float infinity ]
3      ifFalse: [ numerator / denominator ]
```

Listing 4.3: Smalltalk conditional expression.

discuss the design guidelines and maybe replace the rule with an antipodal one that will detect constructs similar to Listing 4.2 and suggest to implement them as in Listing 4.1.

Another FFP use case comes from an analysis of QualityAssistant's impact. The integration of QualityAssistant into Pharo triggered certain changes to the static analysis rules themselves. Developers started to see critiques more often and this motivated them to fix incorrect rules or remove the ones that they found absolutely useless. When analyzing the rules that were removed from the Pharo ecosystem, we discovered a rule which was accused of having too many false positives. A more detailed investigation revealed that the critiques reported as false positives are not clearly false. In Smalltalk branching of a control flow is implemented in a functional style with the help of lexical closures. Listing 4.3 contains an example of a conditional expression. The expression denominator = 0 will be evaluated to a boolean object, and depending on the object itself either the true block[*] or the false block will be evaluated.

The rule detected whether the conditional messages have a block as their argument. This rule is especially useful for novices, as they can forget to wrap their conditional expression in square

---

[*]Block is the Smalltalk term for a closure expression. A block definition is surrounded by square brackets.

```
1 | size = 1 ifTrue: ':' ifFalse: 's:'
```

Listing 4.4: Conditional expression without blocks.

brackets, or confuse them with parentheses that create an ordinary expression instead of a block. In most of the cases the overall expression will still work, because any other object evaluated as a block will return itself. However this is not recommended, as the expressions will be instantly evaluated which will slow down execution, may change the state of the program or even result in an exceptional situation. For example if the snippet in Listing 4.3 did not have square brackets, both expressions `Float infinity` and `numerator / denominator` will evaluate on each execution, including the one where `denominator` is zero, which will cause a zero division exception. On the other hand, in certain cases developers prefer to omit blocks if they contain only a single literal as demonstrated in Listing 4.4. Further analysis showed that the reports about false positives came from experienced developers who are familiar with the implementation of the conditional expression and do not want to see warnings when they omit blocks. The precision of the rule could be improved to ignore the cases where literals are used as the arguments of conditional expressions. Nevertheless, we argue that the rule in its current state brings more value than the burden caused by the false positive critiques. First of all, novices can learn about the design of the conditional expressions and fix their code as soon as they forget to wrap parameters of the conditional expression with blocks. On the other hand it is not hard for experienced developers to simply ignore the critiques if they omit blocks because such hacks are not common. Furthermore, originally in Smalltalk other objects were not polymorphic with the evaluation protocol of the block class, which means that a conditional expression without blocks will not run in all Smalltalk dialects. In other words, this case is similar to the Java/C + + code conventions that suggest to always use brackets around the contents of if-statements [King et al. 1999].

Another especially irritating rule that developers did not like was detecting "cascading messages" that did not end with the `yourself` message. We explain in details the rule and its caveats in Appendix A.

This rule is a good suggestion for novices who are not aware about the pitfalls of Smalltalk cascades, but it can be absolutely annoying for experienced developers who want a different last message on purpose. While this rule is most often mentioned when developers list false positives or bad rules it cannot be clearly labeled with a negative tag. One of the interviewed developers admitted that maybe the rule is not that bad after all because when he rewrites his code to avoid such critiques, the code becomes more understandable.

The use case with the "missing yourself" rule shows one more situation where a rule that was removed could help novices to learn how the programming language works. Additionally, there is some evidence that the rule may suggest a better coding style. While we cannot claim the importance of the rule with respect to design guidelines, we can definitely conclude that instead of discussing the readability aspect that this rule promotes, the rule was simply deleted due to a false positives claim.

The final use case that we want to discuss is related to a warning against bad practices. Some developers do not like the rule that detects the usage of a reflective API, such as checking the type of an object. Similarly to the previous cases this rule may explain that there are other more appropriate ways to solve general problems without the support of reflectivity, but if the developer knows what she is doing, the rule is identified as distracting. On the other hand, senior developers think that the rule is always useful as it suggests not to use the reflective API during a programming session, and highlights questionable pieces of code during a code review. Once again this rule can be a candidate for removal due to a reasonable number of false positive claims from certain developers, but there are is also a evidence of the rule being useful for another group of developers. This means that either the rule should be applied on a personal basis or there should be a better communication to explain the importance of the rule.

The critiques mentioned in this section perform poorly to some extent. The main issues with these use cases are not caused by false positives but rather by vague design guidelines or poor tool design. In certain cases false positives are also present and the static analysis rules can be updated to eliminate some of the incorrect detections, or to provide a more detailed feedback. Nonetheless, to resolve the main issue a static analysis developer has to approach it from the non-false positive perspective.

4.3.4 False Positive Summary

False positive reports are one of the main issues of static analysis tools. However, sometimes even correct static analysis detections are classified as false positives. This not only skews the statistics of static analysis rules, but also masks the real problems. In this section we provide examples where a static analysis report is not useful, but it is also not a false positive. Together with the examples we show the real issues that should be investigated. Static analysis community risks to miss such issues when labeling everything as a false positive when a developer does not like it.

The FFPs described in this section fall into 3 categories:

Bad timing or tool deficiency: rules in this category usually have 100% precision but some developers do not want to see their reports at the certain moment of time. Most likely these rules can benefit from integration in other tools that are used during a different development timeframe. Improving the user interface of the current tool may also improve the acceptance of the reports. A wide range of rules can suffer from the timing issues, they can be completely not related to functionality like the "missing class comment rule" or can target issues that affect the execution like "debugging code left in methods".

Rules for novices: usually blamed by experienced developers who already know about the caveats that the rules are warning about. These rules may be useful for everyone, but are essential for newcomers who may not know language or project paradigms. Rules for novices usually check for calls to certain classes or for specific code constructs that are often a sign of badly designed code.

Lack of consensus: some rules suggest certain style guides that not all developers agree with. Frequently this happens when developers do not understand the rationale behind the rule. Rules in this category are mostly related to style or to certain patterns in the source code.

The line between the false and the true false positives is very thin. For every true false positive one can add a "Possibly" prefix to the repot description and turn it into a FFP. This way the critique stating "Possibly you should use `assert:equals:` instead of `assert:` and `=`" will never be false. But instead of playing with words we want to emphasize that there are issues with static analysis not related to false positives, and they have to be acknowledged separately. We suggest to identify false positives as the issues where critiques cannot be easily identified because of certain limitations. We also believe that there are cases where a rule suffers from both false positives and issues of a different kind.

At the moment there is much evidence that false positives have a negative impact on the acceptance of static analysis tools. It is complicated to improve a false positive ratio, as usually it is caused by lack of information in the source code. On the other hand we showed that some of the reported false positives are not really false detections, but rather issues of the understandability of quality rules, static analysis tool design, or inconsistency in guidelines. These issues can be easier to tackle and thus static analysis developers may improve the acceptance of their tools, by addressing the non-false positive issues first.

4.4 Live Feedback Evaluation

Usage of static analysis is controversial: while it can help to maintain software, it is not commonly used. Besides being common knowledge, the static analysis usage trends are backed by interviews with developers [Johnson et al. 2013] and software repository mining [Beller et al. 2016]. On the other hand, we witnessed an increased usage of static analysis in Pharo after the integration of QualityAssistant. As there was already an on-demand static analyzer, we suspect that the liveness of QualityAssistant played the key role in such a positive acceptance. This hypothesis nicely harmonizes with software developers' opinion established by related research [Yamashita and Moonen 2013].

According to the first survey about QualityAssistant that we described in section 4.2, 90% of Pharo developers find it useful to some extent. The design of QualityAssistant forces developers to constantly use it, because it intrusively provides static analysis feedback and it is integrated into the main development browser. In contrast, the on-demand static analyzer CriticBrowser that was shipped with Pharo for many years, was rarely used by the developers. According to the CriticBrowser usage survey that we discussed in section 4.1, only a quarter of Pharo developers used the analyzer at least once a day, and another quarter used it on a weekly basis. Based on these results we can say that QualityAssistant was a crucial step to make Pharo developers use static analysis, and we believe that our experience can be valuable to boost static analysis usage in other development ecosystems. However, the usage information that we obtained from the two surveys cannot be used to explain why there is such a good acceptance ratio towards QualityAssistant.

After QualityAssistant existed for half a year in a development Pharo image and from a couple months to half of a year in a released Pharo version, we conducted a series of interviews. We interviewed 14 early adopters of a new version of the Pharo IDE that comes with integrated QualityAssistant to understand how they use the live feedback and what are the pros and cons of QualityAssistant and the quality rules that it uses. We also tried to assess the impact that QualityAssistant had on the developers since it was introduced into their workflows. The interviewees identified integration and immediate feedback to be very important for them, which supports the claims of prior research. Additionally, we discovered that developers like the static analysis feedback because it keeps them alert, saves them from expensive errors, motivates them to write better code, and creates synergies with the other practices to preserve software maintainability. There are already enough capable algorithms in the static analysis domain that provide useful information, but our findings show that the feedback has to be live and integrated into IDEs to improve developer experience. We also discovered that in our setup, static analysis plays an educational role, as novice developers can learn about the patterns and idioms of the programming language of used frameworks. Furthermore our static analysis architecture allows framework developers to ship custom static analysis rules with their projects taking the documentation feature to the next level and helping their users to quickly learn about the framework policies.

On the negative side interviewees identified three main problems: vague explanations of critiques, false positives, and deficiencies in the user interface. Because of vague explanations developers lose time while trying to understand the exact problem that a critique tries to address. The feedback about the design of the user interface of QualityAssistant is controversial because, while some developers find it inefficient, others provided scenarios where the design helps them to quickly identify important reports or false positives. Some of the interviewees identified insignificant static analysis rules. Based on their feedback we can summarize that the significance of a rule is a subjective property. We discovered that some developers may prefer to see feedback of certain rules in a different timeframe, for example at commit time as opposed to live feedback. This suggests that instead of focusing on a single timeframe to report all the static analysis detections, we need diverse tools throughout the development process that can provide the same kind of analysis, and that allow static analysis users to decide when exactly they want to see the reports.

In this section we explain our interview setup and reflect on the obtained responses. Our finding are unique in a way that we collected the user experience of the programmers whose main development tool got augmented with live code quality feedback. Our insights can be important for the communities willing to integrate automatic static analysis into their workflows.

4.4.1 Interview Setup

Our main goal is to identify how live static analysis feedback influences the productivity of software developers as opposed to on-demand analyzers. This is a challenging task, as one could run a controlled experiment where two groups of developers use live and on-demand tools to ensure the quality of a project that they have to develop. However, even if the on-demand tool does a better job, there is a high chance that in reality software developers will not use it. We decided to go another way by integrating a live static analysis feedback into a code editor that developers use to ensure that they see code critiques while programming. We followed a *sequential exploratory design* [Creswell and Vicki 2006] and started with a quantitative survey on the usefulness of various features of

QualityAssistant. After obtaining about 90% of a positive feedback about QualityAssistant, we performed a qualitative investigation to explain previous quantitative findings. We designed an interview with open-ended questions, to explore what exactly developers like or dislike about QualityAssistant and the quality rules that it uses, and to assess the impact of the tool on its users.

Selection of Participants

We interviewed developers who used QualityAssistant for at least a few months during their common development tasks. Most of the interviewees were participants of the Pharo Days conference[*] as this is an event that attracts experienced Pharo users. We also interviewed a few Ph.D. students who are using Pharo in their research.

Establishing the Background

To better understand the interview results and understand how comparable they are with the related research, we assessed the overall programming experience of the participants as well as their knowledge about the concept of code smells and related tools by asking them to provide the following information:

1. their current occupation;

2. number of years of programming experience;

3. programming languages that they used for industrial or academic projects;

4. number of years of programming experience in Pharo;

5. their criteria for good code and knowledge of code smells;

6. experience with static analysis tools.

---

[*]https://medium.com/concerning-pharo/pharo-days-2016-c52fe4d7caf

Evaluating QualityAssistant

To assess QualityAssistant we relied on the experience that our interviewees had during their casual work with Pharo 5, as it comes with QualityAssistant preinstalled. We identified three main topics that we wanted to evaluate and based the research questions on them.

- **RQ1** — *what are the positive and negative features of Quality-Assistant?* During the previous survey we identified that 90% of developers like QualityAssistant to some extent, but we wanted to hear which features they find especially useful and useless in their daily job.

- **RQ2** — *what are the good and bad quality rules?* After the QualityAssistant integration we helped to implement a few domain specific rules and saw a removal of some other rules. We wanted to see which rules do developers like and dislike to understand if we are moving in the right direction.

- **RQ3** — *what is the impact of QualityAssistant on the users?* Before the interview we already knew that the vast majority of the QualityAssistant users like it, and that the live feedback motivated certain changes in the quality rule base of Pharo. Additionally, we wanted to understand if QualityAssistant had any impact on the individuals, because we expected that the developers who constantly see the code quality reports will improve their coding skills over time.

To obtain the answers to the listed questions we performed interviews in the form of a discussion where we asked the interviewees how they use QualityAssistant, what do they think about it, *etc.* Then we asked additional questions to help the interview participants reveal the details of their opinion. For example if an interviewee identified false positives as an issue, we asked her to elaborate which rules produced the false critiques. We avoided asking direct questions. For example, there was a case when we asked a developer what does she think about QualityAssistant and the developer answered that the tool is very helpful and she tries to resolve most of the reported critiques. After such an answer we did

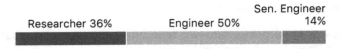

Figure 4.11: Occupation of the interview participants.

not have to ask about the impact of QualityAssistant on the interviewee any more. We asked exact questions only when developers did not mention anything relevant by themselves and usually the responses in such cases did not bring anything new.

4.4.2 Interview Results

In this section, we discuss the lessons learned from the interview responses and summarize them into a few concepts. We also include the responses of developers that did not follow the interview structure but give us valuable insights.

Developers' Background

We recorded 14 interviews of an average length of 14 minutes. The majority of the interviewees with 64% are *engineers*, while the remaining 36% are *researchers* as shown in Figure 4.11. We consider 14% of the interview participants to be *"senior" engineers* as besides doing engineering tasks they are also consulting or supervising other engineers.

The overall software development experience of the interview participants is summarized in Figure 4.12. We asked the interviewees to estimate their industrial experience or in case of academics (and PhD students) we also included time that they spent on programming during their doctoral and postdoctoral studies. Many of the interview participants claimed to have been "programming since high school" but we tried to consider only the post-university experience. A high proportion of 36% of participants have more than *twenty years* of programming experience and 21% — more than *ten years* of experience. Only 14% of the interviewees have programmed for less than *five years*. We believe that the high number of experienced developers is beneficial for the interview, as they may provide more reliable feedback.

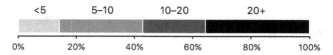

Figure 4.12: Software development experience of interview participants in years.

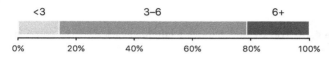

Figure 4.13: Experience of the interviewees with Pharo development environment in years.

At the time the interviews took place Pharo had existed for six years. We explicitly asked the interviewees for their experience in Pharo, as this environment underwent significant changes over the last years and we wanted to understand how QualityAssistant fits into their workflow. As shown on Figure 4.13, only 14% of the participants have used Pharo for less than *three years*, 21% used Pharo for more than *six years* meaning that they are either core developers who worked on it from the beginning or especially interested individuals. The remaining 65% are fairly experienced developers who developed in Pharo from *three to six years*.

Figure 4.14 summarizes the most used programming languages among the interview participants. *Java* is the most popular language with 79% of interview participants being experienced in it. *Python* and *C++* share the second place while being used by 27% of the interviewees and 21% also have experience of programming in *C*, *Javascript* and *Lisp*. Many of the participants mentioned that at the time when they started to work as a programmer "it was not important in which language they developed".

Figure 4.15 summarizes the most common aspects of good code according to the opinion of the interviewees. The criteria are not mutually exclusive because we wanted to record their exact opinions. More than two thirds of the interview participants stated that good code is *easy to read* and *easy to understand*. We believe that these statements are so popular because developers spend signifi-

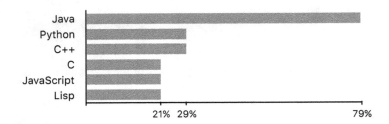

Figure 4.14: Top six programming languages used by the interviewees for software development.

cant amount of time on reading code [Singer et al. 1997]. Some of the developers went into more detail and said that good code can be understood just by reading it without delving into the implementation details. We assume that both criteria refer to the same general feature: being able to understand what a piece of code is doing with as little effort as possible. Another common broad definition stated that good code *respects well-known paradigms* of a programming language, frameworks or even a single project.

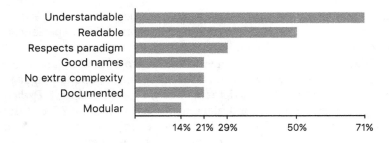

Figure 4.15: Top aspects of good code according to the interviewees.

More precisely developers identified that good code is *modular* and uses *good names*. In conjunction they mentioned that good code uses good abstractions. Another important feature of good code is the *absence of any additional complexity* besides the essential one. Some developers believe that the availability of good *documentation* is another prerequisite of good code. The interviewees also mentioned properties such as: extensible, concise, well-tested, continuously integrated, maintainable, and clean. Some participants stated that the definition of good code is context-dependent. For example efficient bit-shifting operations may be hard to understand by reading the code itself, but could be well-documented. In fact the responses of the interviewees highly correlate with the maintainability aspect of the ISO software quality standard [ISO/IEC 2010]. Software maintainability is composed of analyzability, modifiability, testability, reusability, and modularity. Not only did the interviewees mention exactly some of those maintainability subcategories, but also other criteria like good names and paradigm adherence are prerequisites for maintainability.

All interview participants knew about code smells, and except for one person, everybody had used some kind of static analysis tools to detect code quality issues. Such a high percentage of developers knowing about code smells is uncommon when compared to related research [Yamashita and Moonen 2013], and may result from the high number of experienced engineers that participated in our interview, or from the code quality culture present in Pharo and Smalltalk in general. About half of the interviewees used CriticBrowser — the static analysis tool that we discussed in section 4.1. There was no other particular tool that was used by a significant number of participants. However they mentioned using *Java tools* like Checkstyle and PMD, *lint tools* like PyLint and JSLint, *IDEs with quality reports* like IntelliJ, PHPStorm, Eclipse, CodeBlocks and SonarCube on an integration server.

QualityAssistant Feedback

This subsection discusses the responses of the interviewees and highlights important lessons related to RQ1 (what are the positive and negative features of QualityAssistant?). All but one of the interview participants provided some kind of positive feedback summarized in Figure 4.16.

More than half of interviewees mentioned that *live feedback* of QualityAssistant is highly beneficial. While speaking about this feature they also mentioned that having an integrated tool that without a special setup runs automatically is crucial. As mentioned before, the live feedback in Pharo uses exactly the same quality

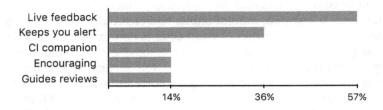

Figure 4.16: Top positive feedback topics.

rules that are employed by standalone tools and CI. Although the CI process of Pharo itself uses a subset of rules dedicated to critical errors and style conventions to speed up the validation and avoid the noise caused by informative rules. One of the developers noticed that QualityAssistant operates on a small scope: the method or class that a developer is currently working on. This speeds up the feedback and shortens the time between changes made to code and detection of an issue. For example, the developer mentioned that running static analysis on the complete project he is working on takes about 10 minutes, while QualityAssistant can provide an immediate feedback about the code you are currently working on. Similarly about a quarter of the developers noted that QualityAssistant can be used as a *sidekick of a CI server*. They said that sometimes you need to wait a significant amount of time while a CI server is validating the project, just to find out that you have made a mistake which you have to resolve before submitting the patch again. On the other hand QualityAssistant performs analysis immediately as a developer browses or changes code. Thanks to the live feedback, mistakes can be detected in an early stage and instantly resolved, thus significantly cutting down the waiting time in comparison with a CI server. Our findings greatly support the need of integration of static analysis into the development workflow previously suggested by other studies [Beller et al. 2016; Sadowski et al. 2015]. And while related research has claimed that static analysis should be integrated at least on the level of CI validation [Beller et al. 2016], we argue that integration into development tools further increases the benefits. This supports the prior interviews where developers expressed the need to see the static analysis feedback as soon as possible [Yamashita and Moonen 2013]. Additionally, previous research did not consider static analysis as a part of an ecosystem, while in our case some developers found QualityAssistant to be useful in combination with the CI Server.

Lesson 1. Integration and out-of-the-box functionality of static analysis is highly important for a good acceptance, while live feedback makes it more user friendly.

Lesson 2. Static analysis should not be concentrated in a single tool. CI server can ensure global rule adherence while live editor feedback provides a quick guidance.

More than one third of the participants noticed that Quality-Assistant *keeps them alert* and has saved them a few times when they made a mistake, which is hard to spot immediately, but may cause unexpected behavior in the future. These people estimated that while traditional debugging could take them up to 15 minutes, QualityAssistant pointed out the issue immediately. Some developers stated that QualityAssistant *makes them think* more about the code and in this way encourages them to make their code better. This applies to the warnings about missing documentation, usage of low-level and reflective APIs and usage of side effects. Two developers mentioned that sometimes critiques of QualityAssistant are annoying but in a good way, because the developers are encouraged to improve their code and make it more understandable for the others, which is beneficial in long term. The senior developers who are part of Pharo patch review process said that QualityAssistant *guides code reviews* by highlighting questionable pieces of code and detecting general issues while allowing them to focus on more important questions. The problem of reviewers focusing on the easy parts and missing real issues was previously identified by Bacchelli and Bird [Bacchelli and Bird 2013]. Now we can confirm that static analysis aids code reviewers in their work. Moreover, sometimes developers simply inspect code while searching for something, and see certain critiques that can be instantly resolved as the developer is already focused on that piece of code.

Lesson 3. Developers like the live feedback because it motivates them to write better code and keeps them alert about the possible mistakes or highlights suspicious parts of code during a review.

There were few common points regarding the negative feedback. These issues are presented in Figure 4.17. According to the interviewees *false positives* were one of the most important problems. On the other hand false positives were never perceived as the most severe issue. The interview participants acknowledged that false positives are an essential part of static analysis and that an obvious solution is to remove the responsible rules, but then you also lose some important critiques. They also acknowledged that false positives are very distracting in a standalone setup, where you need to review hundreds of reports many of which are false positives. However in the live feedback setup they had to focus only on a few reports and false positives did not cause significant problems. Previously, a static analysis team at Facebook discovered that reports related to a patch under code review are better received by the developers, as they recently worked in the context of the submitted patch [Calcagno et al. 2015]. Based on the experience of our developers live feedback benefits even more from the developer context.

Lesson 4. Standalone tools usually generate all the reports about a project at once and this complicates identification of false positives. Live feedback eases this burden by scoping the reports to a current context.

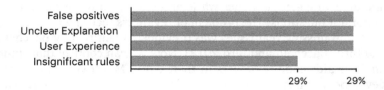

Figure 4.17: Top negative feedback topics.

Another common issue was related to *insignificant rules*. Some developers stated that they are not interested in critiques of the rules that detect uncommented classes or the usage of reflection-related APIs. While this category of issues is often merged with false positives, we analyze it separately, according to the definitions discussed in section 4.3. We noticed that the attitude towards false positives and insignificant rules greatly depends on the experience of interviewees and their current position. More *experienced developers* who manage teams or review contributions to a project are in *favor of spending extra time* and paying attention to static analysis reports while the participants with fewer years of programming experience and especially Ph.D. students working on their personal projects tend to claim that their project is well-implemented and they do not care about some rules.

Lesson 5. Experienced developers tend to like static analysis more than novice developers who are usually too self-confident to accept criticism.

Some developers identified *unclear explanation* of the critiques as the most severe problem. The problem itself has two parts: the explanation of the critique and localization of the issue in the code. The former happens when the rationale behind a quality rule is not clear and developers cannot understand why their code is bad. The latter issue happens when the critique does not provide enough information to understand what exactly triggered the rule and how to fix it. For example an interviewee mentioned a rule designed to detect deprecated method invocations. However, critiques of that rule were reporting a complete method that was invoking a deprecated functionality thus forcing the developer to check all invocations in the reported method to identify which one of them calls a deprecated functionality. In this case a feedback loop designed similarly to that of Tricorder [Sadowski et al. 2015] can be beneficial as it allows users to quickly notify the static analysis developers if they do not understand a critique.

> *Lesson 6.* Critiques may fail either to explain why a detection is a violation, or to specify which piece of code is violating the rule. This causes big problems for developers. A feedback loop from static analysis users to developers of rules is very helpful in such cases.

Finally, almost one third of developers complained about *user experience*. The interviewees did not like the implementation used for banning critiques. The implementation reuses the strategy of SmallLint where the source code is modified with certain annotations. The developers do not like that something introduces changes into their source code just because they ban the critiques that do not want to see again. However, this issue naturally exists in the SmallLint engine and thus we do not discuss it in this chapter. On the other hand some developers found QualityAssistant's user interface inefficient. One of them did not like that QualityAssistant takes up some space from the code editor. On the other hand, another developer didn't like the fact that they can only see up to three quality critiques at a time. The initially presented critiques may not be as important while the following ones hidden at the bottom in the list may report important issues. Additional study is needed to assess the strengths and weaknesses of the current live feedback design because while some interviewees did not like it, we believe that the current design may prove to be beneficial. In the sub-subsection "Successful Scenario" on page 89 we provide a scenario where the current design supports quick comprehension of critiques.

Rule Usefulness

Despite the high ratio of positive feedback, most of the interview participants struggled to identify the rules that are useful for them. One third of them agreed that good rules are related to a *specific context*, such as a certain project. One developer went into detail and told us that the rules of Glamorous Toolkit[*] were extremely useful for him. Glamorous Toolkit is a project developed externally but integrated and shipped with Pharo. It has its own domain-specific language (DSL) for scripting user interfaces. It also provides

---

[*]http://gtoolkit.org

```
1  aLink := aLinkOrObject asLink
2  self isEmpty ifTrue: [lastLink := aLink].
```

Listing 4.5: Missing statement separation.

SmallLint rules that check the DSL and suggest transformations to enable lazy initialization and so improve the UI performance. By providing its own rules the project educates unfamiliar developers about the best way to use the UI framework.

One developer stated that *style rules* are useful at the beginning, and they help to familiarize developers with the concepts of Pharo, but now he mostly focuses on the rules that point out *possible bugs*. Another developer mentioned that some style rules helped him to avoid accidental mistakes where the source code was syntactically correct, but in fact did not follow the intention of the developer and at the same time resulted in constructs that are not recommended and were detected by quality rules. Consider the example code snippet in Listing 4.5. Two lines were intended to represent two statements, but the period character that serves as the statement delimiter in Smalltalk is omitted from the end of the first line. This results in a single statement where the result of an expression is assigned to the aLink variable. Furthermore the expression consists of a message chain asLink self isEmpty ifTrue: sent to the aLinkOrObject variable. The exception will occur when the result of aLinkOrObject asLink will receive the self message, as it does not implement the self method. However, there is a rule that checks for messages with the self selector and warns that they look suspicious.

Finally even the most negative interview participant who claimed not to pay attention to QualityAssistant at all admitted that there are useful rules that detect invocations of non-existent methods, or unused variables.

The summary of the most common rules identified as "bad" is shown in Figure 4.18. We identified three groups of ineffective rules and each of them was mentioned by about a quarter of the interview participants. One of the bad rule categories consists of rules that are *based on metrics* such as classes with too many methods, methods with too many lines of code, *etc.* Developers reported that most of these issues require significant effort to resolve and usually do not make sense in the setup of QualityAssistant, where you want to have issues that just appear and can be quickly resolved.

Figure 4.18: Negative aspects of rules according to the interviewees.

Another bad category is the group of good rules with *bad timing*. The rules in this category do make sense, but some developers do not want to see the defected violations as soon as they appear. For example ideally your code should not contain debugging statements or unused variables, but if you are in a debugging process some developers do not want to be continuously bothered by the "debugging code rule". We hypothesize, that for such developers the notification about the critiques should be delayed to the moment when the criticized code is not being modified any more. On the other hand some of the developers said that they like those rules and that they treat them as a todo list: you have created a variable, now you have a task to use it. Metric rules are a subcategory of the rules with bad timing, but they were explicitly identified by developers and thus we assigned them to a unique group. Previous research strongly emphasizes the question of *when* is the best time to provide static analysis feedback. Beller *et al.* suggest to do it at least on a CI server [Beller et al. 2016], Sadowski *et al.* claim that a pre-commit period is the perfect time to show the static analysis feedback [Sadowski et al. 2015], and according to the interviews of Yamashita and Moonen — developers want static analysis reports as soon as possible [Yamashita and Moonen 2013]. Based on the collected data we argue that instead of focusing on a *single tool* with a perfect time to display results, we need *many tools* that work on different levels and then we should try to understand which rules should be used by which tool. Moreover, as the timing requirements of the critiques can depend on each individual, we suggest to use a single quality model that is shared by all tools. This way a developer will be able to assign different roles to a preferred time span. For example live feedback such as that offered by QualityAssistant can provide the most crucial reports immediately, while another tool like Tricorder can provide a clean-up feedback (like suggestions to remove a debugging code) before a commit is performed, and a CI server like SonarQube [Campbell and Papapetrou 2013] can include metric-based rules to identify a part of the code that requires additional inspection for the next refactoring session.

Lesson 7. There is no perfect time to display a quality violation to a developer. This time depends both on the kind of violation and on the personal preferences of a developer. We need more configurable options to provide static analysis feedback throughout the development cycle.

The third group refers to *known Pharo idioms* and mostly mimics the rules that we used as the examples of false false positives in section 4.3. They include the *missing yourself* rule and the rule warning about the usage of the reflective API. While discussing this rules some interviewees acknowledged that the critiques in question actually suggest good programming practices, but most of the participants were simply annoyed by these critiques.

Some interview participants did not specify concrete rules, but rather built their answer around the *Foreign function interface (FFI) project.* The Pharo FFI framework is built in such a way that users have to violate some rules in order to use it. These are mostly explanatory and style rules that are violated by FFI's DSL. This use case once again reveals the need for mechanics that can disable some rules only for a certain scope: users of FFI calls in the current case.

Lesson 8. Rules should be scope to a context of a program. Additionally, an external module should be able to silence a more generic rule for the code in the module's context.

We did not find an exact answer to RQ2 (what are the good and bad quality rules?). But we discovered new challenges such as how to display critiques in different tools at different times or how to restrict rules from certain contexts. The only concrete answer for RQ2 is the benefit from the domain-specific rules that come from other projects.

QualityAssistant's Impact on Individuals

All the stories that developers told us while reasoning about the benefits of QualityAssistant contribute to RQ3 (what is the impact of QualityAssistant on the users?). For example, when a developer tells us that QualityAssistant saved him 15 minutes of debugging time, or a student tells us that critiques motivated her to write documentation, we see this as a positive impact that QualityAssistant had on individuals. Half of the interview participants believe that their programming habits changed because of QualityAssistant. Some of them simply enjoy immediately fixing issues reported by QualityAssistant. Other developers use it to guide their code review. But most of the interviewees impacted by QualityAssistant reported learning something new from the tool. Senior developers mostly learned about common style guidelines and approaches to make your code portable across different Smalltalk dialects. On the other hand novice developers were motivated to document their code and learned about optimization techniques and some Pharo-specific paradigms.

While some developers changed their habits to quickly react to issues as soon as they are detected, the main discovery in our opinion are the teaching possibilities of the static analysis tool. Developers actually learn from static analysis despite their experience. For example one teacher shared with us that many of his students tend to compare the equality of a boolean expression to `true` and such a tool could educate them that this is a bad and unneeded practice. On the other hand experienced developers who are new to Pharo learn that instead of using

```
expression1 & expression2
```

they can use

```
expression1 and: [ expression2 ]
```

so the second expression will be evaluated lazily in case the first one returns true. Even experienced Pharo developers can learn about API changes to Pharo itself or some other frameworks that are used in their project. One example for this are the rules of Glamorous Toolkit that suggest how to use the DSL more efficiently. Another example is the API change of the SUnit testing framework that provides a more understandable output if one uses:

```
self assert: actualValue equals: expectedValue
```

instead of:

```
self assert: (actualValue = expectedValue)
```

The classic approach is to read the documentation or the change log. However, documentation tends to be outdated and as a result "source code is more trusted than documentation" [Roehm et al. 2012]. Additionally the approach to learn from documentation expects that a developer has to consume a complete set of knowledge needed for a project and be able to use it at any given time. On the other hand a static analyzer can pinpoint just a related subset of knowledge needed in a certain situation.

Lesson 9. Live static analysis also serves as a documentation that is available in the exact context when you need it.

Successful Scenario

Both the initial survey and the current interviews showed that most developers find that QualityAssistant playing the role of an artificial pair programmer more helpful than distracting. Now we present additional findings that explain how QualityAssistant is used by developers and why they are satisfied to such a high degree.

Two of the experienced interview participants shared their vision of how the developers use QualityAssistant. One of them said:

> *"Sometimes QualityAssistant warns you against using certain meta-programming features, but you have to use them anyway, however the warnings are still useful because it makes you think again about why you did this and warns about possible issues in that context."*

Another person said:

> *"We (experts) are so used to jump over things while trying to understand code, that one or two lines of the critiques do not impose much more distraction."*

The later interviewee also expressed a hypothesis that QualityAssistant can be distracting for novice programmers, as they are not used to quickly skimming over a large amount of information.

We hypothesize that the interface of QualityAssistant greatly contributes to the ability of quickly understanding a critique or discarding it. Critiques are presented as entries in a list and can be read without any additional interface manipulations. Also tiny textual hints at the beginning of the critique description can help a developer to localize the issue without additional actions. Finally we believe that the fact that a developer is presented only with critiques about the code that he is working on, reduces the information pressure. In fact the studied approach is similar to JIT static analysis by Do *et al.* [Do et al. 2016], but we are also leveraging the UI of the Smalltalk Browser when a developer is presented with only one code entity (like a method or a class) at a time. We have informally asked some developers if they would like to have critiques represented as inline highlights of a source code instead of a list at the bottom and they said that currently they like the possibility to quickly read the descriptions, or ignore the critiques altogether by simply not looking at the bottom bar. According to previous studies, static analysis tools for Java detect on average 40 issues for every thousand lines of code [Heckman and Williams 2008] while an average Java or C++ method has ten lines of code [Lanza and Marinescu 2006]. This means that while working on a method a developer would encounter on average 0.4 critiques. We believe that while a developer is focused on a certain context, he does not require much time to look at one more line of text and deciding whether to act on it or ignore it.

Lesson 10. Static analysis feedback is easier to deal with if it is related to the context a developer is working on and she can skim through it without having to interact too much with the UI.

Drawbacks of Scoped Feedback

While almost none of our interviewees mentioned the issues of scoped feedback, we want to share our own experience. There are certain issues that may appear outside of the scope that is being changed. For example if a developer removes the last reference to an instance variable, class or another resource there is no way to warn them that the resource is not used anymore as it resides in another scope. In other words, CriticBrowser is not a competitor of QualityAssistant and each of them performs better in a certain context. Of course one can implement a more complex analysis that checks how changes in the current context would affect the rest of the system, but this requires additional computation time and special means to display reports. This issue is not critical for scoped feedback, but should be taken into account.

4.4.3 Usefulness for Novices

During this interview, two contradictory thoughts emerged. One of them suggests that QualityAssistant may overwhelm novice developers with different critiques, while the other one says that novices are actually learning from this tool. To shed light on this question we surveyed the master students of a Software Modeling and Analysis course to identify whether QualityAssistant was useful to them. For most of the students this was their first encounter with Pharo, thus we find the selected group of participants to well represent the *novice developers* category. To avoid bias, we did not offer any reward for the survey participation and we allowed students to stay anonymous. Seven students participated in the survey and only one student knew Pharo for half a year before the course. Five of the students had an average of $1.8 \pm 1 (M \pm SD)$ years of industrial development experience. We asked students to evaluate the usefulness of QualityAssistant on a 7-point Likert scale: *1. very useful, 2. useful, 3. sometimes useful, 4. not influential, 5. sometimes disturbing, 6. disturbing, or 7. very disturbing.*

The responses are presented in Figure 4.19. It is worth noticing that all the students claimed that QualityAssistant was useful for them, which refutes the assumption that novices are overwhelmed and confused by live static analysis feedback. In the freeform feedback the students specified that QualityAssistant taught them about the functionality that they did not know before as well as some programming concepts of Pharo. On the negative side a student reported the user interface to be user-unfriendly, and found some critique explanations hard to understand. Two of the students specified that they also found other live static analyzers to be useful in their previous experience with the IntelliJ IDEA and ReSharper.

Figure 4.19: Usefulness of QualityAssistant from students perspective.

4.4.4 Threats to Validity

Internal Validity

The semi-structured interviews were performed by the developer of QualityAssistant. The interviewer did his best not to lead or influence the interviewees. Additionally, QualityAssistant is integrated into Pharo, which should motivate the participants to provide true information and not simply make the interviewer happy. However, we cannot exclude the existence of biased answers. To minimize the effects of this threat we tried to focus more on the stories that interviewees were telling about their experience with QualityAssistant rather than qualitative feedback where they tried to assess whether something is good or bad.

While all the participants work with Pharo, some of them use either an older version of Pharo or even a completely different language for their main job. This may introduce some bias, as these participants may not be using Pharo with QualityAssistant as their main development tool in their daily work.

External Validity

While Pharo is similar to other object-oriented languages such as Java, Python or Objective-C, there are certain differences, particularly related to its support of live programming, that may not be generalizable. Similarly, QualityAssistant does not have many conceptual differences in comparison with other similar tools. However, we expect that there may be bias on the "community level". For example the Pharo and Smalltalk community in general expects a dedicated IDE that will assist in debugging, refactoring, *etc.* On the other hand, there are communities that would rather take a simplistic but extensible editor like EMACS [Stallman 1981] and add other tools on their own. We believe that our interviewees had significantly high programming experience, and worked with different technologies through their career to provide reasonable feedback.

All our participants were aware of the concept of code smells. This differs from the population considered by other research [Yamashita and Moonen 2013; Bessey et al. 2010], which means that our findings should not be directly compared with others.

The interface of QualityAssistant is simplistic and did not undergo any significant design activities. Moreover, while the functionality of QualityAssistant is similar to other quality tools no two tools are created equal. This may introduce some bias when generalizing our finding to the other available tools. Additional study is required to assess how different quality tool interfaces perform against each other.

The result of our study should not be generalized to all kinds of static analysis. The quality rules that were used by QualityAssistant are comparable to those of FindBugs, PyLint, and JSHint — the tools used in similar studies. And while we claim that live feedback brings the context closer to a reported critique and helps developers to deal with false positives this does not mean that any kind of analysis will be useful in our setup. For example there are certain categories of rules with a high rate of false positives that are hard to validate making the rules rarely usable. Providing the feedback of such rules immediately should speed up the critique analysis, but this may still not be enough to make the rules usable.

4.4.5 Conclusions

In this section we present an experience report about a live static analysis feedback integrated into an IDE based on 14 interviews with industrial and academic participants. Our results show that live feedback is highly beneficial, as it brings up possible issues at the time when a programmer is looking at code and thus reduces the time needed to get into the context of a critique. This result supports the claim that was previously made based on the wishes expressed by developers in another study. We also confirm that integration plays an important role. And while other research suggests to integrate static analysis on the level of CI validation, we claim that even more benefit can be achieved by integrating static analysis into a development environment. Additionally, we discovered that live feedback in an IDE can complement a pre-integration check on CI.

Live static analysis reports worked well in our case and can be easily achieved by taking existing rules, and displaying critiques in a code editor. Nevertheless we discovered that not all developers like to be immediately bothered with all available critiques. Based on our use cases we believe that there should be multiple reporting tools available throughout the development process that can use a unified static analysis model. This way a developer will be able to decide in which timeframe she wants to see the critiques of a certain rule.

We also discovered that many developers learn from static analysis feedback. Novices learn basic programming guidelines and patterns of the programming language while more experienced developers learn about optimization tricks and portability guidelines. As some static analysis rules may come from other projects such as frameworks and libraries, the developers can learn different features of the projects including the changes that happened to APIs. However, for this approach to work the developer of a framework has to be sure that its users will see the critiques. This additionally motivates integration of static analysis into IDEs.

We conducted our study on Pharo, which has an experienced but small community. We are also fortunate that the Pharo Board integrated QualityAssistant into an IDE used by real developers for their business needs, as this allowed us to run the experiment. Nevertheless we believe that other programmers also deserve development environments with a live static analysis feedback. We hope that our study will motivate IDE vendors to implement such integration, especially as there are already many useful open-source static analysis rules for different languages.

We confirmed that integration is an important prerequisite for static analysis. Sadly, there are still many studies that focus on standalone tools and render them as not welcome or not efficient, although they may perform much better when integrated. We are looking forward to studies on advanced static analysis aspects such as usage of machine learning to provide a personalized feedback, or approaches on dealing with time and scope constraints.

The Impact on the Ecosystem

We integrated QualityAssistant— the live intrusive code quality feedback into the core Pharo distribution. Based on the data collected from the Pharo developers' impressions and experience, we can say that QualityAssistant is a crucial feature needed by the developers for a long time. While the user satisfaction is an important goal of any product, we believe that human judgment is subjective and should be accompanied by another source of assessment to form conclusions. In this chapter we analyze the impact that QualityAssistant had on the Pharo ecosystem itself.

First of all we encountered a problem while analyzing the quality evolution of the complete codebase during Pharo 5 development. The quality rules were changed many times during the development of the new version of Pharo. As a result the quality evolution was based on a measure that was continuously changing. To overcome this issue we devised a three dimensional visualization that decomposes quality variations caused by changes in code from those caused by changes in rules. We present the visual approach in section 5.1. Afterwards, in section 5.2 we analyze the changes that happened to the rules to understand how QualityAssistant influenced them.

5.1 3D Decomposition of Quality Evolution Anomalies

In chapter 4 we described how QualityAssistant was integrated into Pharo, was positively accepted by the developers, and according to the interview helped some developers to avoid annoying bugs or even taught them a thing or two. Afterwards we decided to investigate how the quality evolution of the Pharo project changed after QualityAssistant was integrated. By quality evolution we mean the changes in the number of critiques about the source code of Pharo by the rules present in the system. At the beginning of our analysis, we did not consider the fact that the rules can also change to better capture the expectations towards the project. The rule evolution complicates the analysis because instead of analyzing only the evolution of the project's quality, one also has to account for the changes to the project's requirements. For example, consider a version n that contains 5 critiques from a rule that was removed (together with its critiques) in the version $n + 1$. The removal of 5 critiques in the new version was not caused by improvements in the code but rather by changes in the quality measure: the rules.

While not realizing the fact of rule evolution we tried to identify which changes happened to the critiques through the development history of Pharo 5. We encountered versions where the number of changed critiques was as high as 5% of the total number of methods in the software system. We manually examined these anomalies and detected that in one of them a rule was fixed to include the violations that it was previously ignoring. Another anomaly was caused by unloading of a big module.

We could not relate the observed anomalies to a single cause, which restricted us from using already available visual and statistical methods. To understand the nature of our data set we created a visualization that uses the changes between quality values as building blocks and lays them out in three dimensions: *software components, quality rules* and *software versions*. The visualization relies on the sparse nature of the data, and pre-attentive clustering possibilities of human brain to quickly detect the anomalies. This approach allowed us to see a high level overview of our data set, distinguish the anomalies caused by rule changes from the ones caused

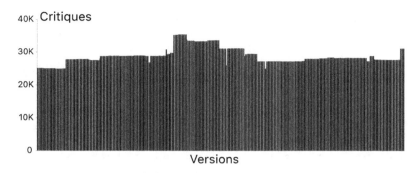

Figure 5.1: Critiques histogram.

by software changes and finally clean the data of the anomalies. Moreover with our approach we identified a dozen anomalies that reveal bad practices or wrong design decisions and can be valuable for the decision makers behind the Pharo development.

The dataset that we analyzed with the 3D decomposition approach was published and is available online [Tymchuk et al. 2016b]. To demonstrate our visualization in action, we recorded a video, which is available via the following link:
https://youtu.be/GJ8BONoaF0Q.

5.1.1 Problem Description

The development cycle of Pharo 5 lasted for one year during which 680 incremental updates (also known as versions or patches) took place. During this period, Pharo developers had CriticBrowser — an on-demand static analysis tool with 124 rules at their disposal. A subset of these rules was used by a CI server to validate newly proposed patches. In the middle of the Pharo 5 development cycle, QualityAssistant was integrated and developers started to see live critiques by the SmallLint rules in their code editor.

Running SmallLint on all versions in this development cycle produces around 19.5 million violations. Figure 5.1 shows the total number of critiques per each version. Many of the critiques are related to essential complexity [Brooks 1995] and never change. The number of critiques that were added or removed from version to version is around 64.5 thousands. Inspection of the plot quickly reveals many versions where the number of critiques changed by as many as 5 000 or 15% from the version's total. We refer to these changes as *anomalies* because according to our investigation they are clear outliers and are unlikely to have been caused by a common refactoring or feature implementation.

During the manual investigation of a few anomalies we analyzed the data from the versioning system to understand which source code changes caused the anomalies. Additionally we analyzed the issue tracker entries linked to the software patches to understand what was the reason behind the changes. We discovered that in some cases developers were fixing a faulty rule, cleaning code of certain critiques, or simply applying a refactoring. Here we provide an example of the anomalies that we selectively inspected:

1. An increase of 5 000 critiques, all of which were reported by a single rule responsible for detecting unused methods. Previously the rule was broken. After a fix it reported all 5'000 unused methods. The anomaly does not represent a change in quality: the methods were present previously, but not reported. The anomaly itself can be interesting for stakeholders to learn about improvements happening to the quality support system and their impact.

2. A decrease of 1 000 critiques caused by a removal of a big module that was implementing low-level functionality. The anomaly represents a change in quality, as the removal of a module simplifies maintenance of the whole project. On the other hand the change is mostly related to essential complexity and is not useful when included on the same level with common changes.

3. Another decrease of 2 500 critiques was caused by developers troubleshooting reports caused by a single rule. The anomaly is caused by intentional changes in the source code and raises a question: "when and why were these critiques introduced and why were they not addressed earlier?"

4. 2'500 critiques were added for multiple reasons: (a) one rule was fixed, as previously it was including false-positive results;

(b) a new rule was added; (c) a new version of a package management module was integrated. Multiple types of changes that could significantly affect the number of critiques made it very hard to reason about the anomaly.

Additionally, around 90% of all rules were changed to some degree. Not all the changes affected the functionality. They could be related to the changes of a description, group, severity, or could be caused by a refactoring of the critique detection algorithm.

Detecting the anomalies from the chart in Figure 5.1 may seem easy, but not all the critiques of an affected version are related to an anomaly, and we want to keep the "innocent" critiques for further analysis. Moreover one version can have multiple anomalies of different types that should be handled separately. We acknowledge that some statistical methods may help to identify the anomalies, but at the moment we are not aware of the "anatomy" of anomalies, thus we want to obtain an overview with the help of visualization.

After analyzing the selected anomalies and other aspects of the data set we compiled the requirements for analyzing the impact of the quality analysis tools. Critique evolution consists of two types of changes: *gradual* and *extreme*. The former are the result of common code evolution that slightly impacts the critiques on each commit. We can analyze gradual changes by using graphical and statistical methods and draw conclusions based on the trend of changes. However, the latter consist of anomalies. It is complicated to provide an evolutionary summary for them as extreme changes are diverse and not frequent. The previous inspections revealed that the anomalies are caused by critiques that represent a single rule in one version, or are related to a single package in one version. We believe that a report about extreme changes should consist of summaries that describe each individual anomaly. Additionally we need a possibility to analyze the data on a time scale and correlate an anomaly with similar ones that have occurred in other versions.

5.1.2   Related Work

Our visualization approach is driven by the characteristics of our data set. In our first attempt we used a simple bar chart (as demonstrated on Figure 5.1). Thus, to understand the behavior of each package and each group of rules we had to create separate charts. We could detect versions, and packages revealing high changes in the number of rules. However, we could not identify the reason behind the anomaly, as in the chart both package changes and rule changes are projected onto a single dimension.

The ChronoTwigger [Ens et al. 2014] visualization supports the analysis of two co-changing properties. However, it is constrained to properties in the same dimension, and in our case we needed to analyze the evolution of critiques based on two evolving parameters: packages and rules.

The Evolution Matrix [Lanza and Ducasse 2002] technique, uses polymetric views to visualize the evolution of software packages over the time. We visualized the number of critiques and number of rules from where the critiques originated as the metrics on the rectangles' extents. We found that the Evolution matrix provided a good overview of the relation between packages and versions. Although this gave us a better understanding about the places with significantly higher number of critiques from diverse rules, we could not investigate the reason behind the anomalies.

To assess the benefit of visualizing package-rule relations, we created an incidence matrix. In it, one axis represented packages while another one represented rules. The only metric that we applied to matrix cells was the number of changed critiques represented as an amount of blue coloring. We produced several samples for data coming from different versions. They revealed patterns that helped us to identify abnormal changes of critiques. Figure 5.2 shows part of the visualization of *version 241*, where critiques have changed in many packages, but for only one rule.

2-dimensional matrices were already used to visually solve diverse time-related problems. The Small MultiPiles [Bach et al. 2015] approach clusters similar matrices from the history into piles and presents them as small multiples. Brandes and Nick use glyphs based on gestaltlines [Brandes et al. 2013] to represent an evolution between relations in an incidence matrix [Brandes and Nick 2011]. Finally AniMatrix [Rufiange and Melançon 2014] uses animated matrix cells to convey the evolutionary information. While these approaches looked promising we found them difficult to use with our dataset because matrix cells were as small as 2.5mm or 10px in width and height when the matrix was fully expanded on a 27 inch

Figure 5.2: An incidence matrix to visualize change of critiques.

display. Additionally our main concern was to detect anomalies in the project's evolution instead of sequential patterns. We believed that seeing the correlation between packages, rules and versions in one image will solve this problem. Thus, we explored a visualization that uses a 3-dimensional metaphor.

We reviewed Sv3D [Marcus et al. 2003] which uses a 3D representation. In it, data is depicted by cylinders that are positioned using three numerical attributes of data. One extra attribute is mapped to the height of cylinders. Finally, cylinders are colored to encode a categorical attribute. Although we found it useful to provide an overview, it did not help us to identify anomalies since occlusion among cylinders hindered our ability to identify anomalies in the data.

Matrix Cubes [Bach et al. 2014] is a visualization technique based on a space-time cube metaphor of stacked adjacency matrices in chronological order. Since we have to analyze the relation between objects of different kind, we adopted this technique and expand it to use incidence matrices.

5.1.3 Visualization Approach

Our visualization is developed in Pharo itself using a 3D version of Roassal [Bergel 2016] — an agile visualization engine. While we believe that our approach is applicable in many different contexts, we decided to script the exact visualization that we need instead of building a highly customizable application. This is why our main

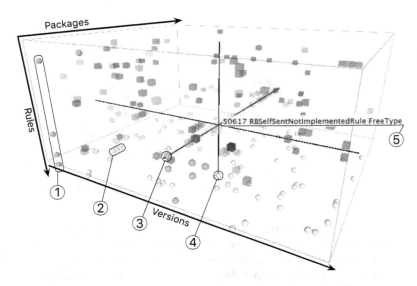

Figure 5.3: Visualization Example. Aligned changes of rules ① and packages ②. Crosshair penetrates spheres that represent changes in a rule ③ and a package ④. A popup ⑤ appears with detail when hovering over an element.

focus is on the explanation of the general approach and discussion of the details that may work differently for other cases.

Our data set can be indexed with triples of the form: *package name, rule name; version number*. We want to study a metric called the *critique delta*: an integer value that represents the number of critiques that have changed in a *package* based on a *rule* in a *version*. A critique delta of version v is calculated by subtracting the number of critiques in version $v-1$ from the number of critiques in version v.

As we wanted to build a visualization based on three independent values, we decided to use a 3-dimensional space and encode the critique delta values with the help of color intensity. An example of the visualization is presented in Figure 5.3.

Critique deltas are represented as cubes in a 3D matrix. Versions are natural numbers, and we sort them in an ascending order to represent data in a historical way. Also we sort packages and rules in an alphabetical order. First of all they are represented in this order in many tools that are used inside an IDE that makes this ordering a common way to comprehend them. Secondly, multiple packages form implicit groups by beginning with common prefixes. Alphabetic ordering keeps implicit package groups together and enhances comprehension as it is common for these groups to co-evolve at the same time.

Hovering over cubes displays a popup (⑤ in Figure 5.3) with information about the cube and a *crosshair* that allows a user to identify which entities are at the same level as the one being hovered over.

We believe our visualization technique is general enough to tackle problems of other domains. Therefore, we classify it using the five dimensions proposed by Maletic *et al.* [Maletic et al. 2002]. The *task* tackled by our visualization is identification of anomalies and cleaning of data; the *audience* consists of software analysts who need to make sense of quality evolution; the *target* is a data set containing a set of critique rules for each package of a range of revisions; the *representation* used can be classified as a geometrically-transformed projection according to Keim's taxonomy [Keim and Kriegel 1996]); the *medium* used to display the visualization is a high-resolution monitor with at least 2560 x 1440 pixels.

We designed our visualization according to the visualization mantra introduced by Shneidermann [Shneiderman 1996]. First, users obtain an *overview* to identify places of interest. Once they find one, they *zoom* in to have details, they can also *filter* surrounding data to maximize the focus on the objects of interest, and finally they can obtain *details-on-demand* of the critiques delta of a package within a version.

Coloring

We use color coding to determine if the critiques delta is positive or negative. Red represents an increased number of critiques, while blue means that the number of critiques has decreased in that version. Translucency of cubes is determined based on the absolute value of the critique delta: the cube with the biggest absolute critiques delta value will be opaque, while the one with no changes will be transparent. The other cubes will have their translucency proportional to the maximum of absolute values of the critiques deltas. This ensures that the larger changes will have more visual impact in comparison with the smaller ones.

We considered two approaches for calculating translucency: one of them calculates a separate maximum for each version, while another one uses a single maximum based on all the critique deltas. The former approach ensures that in case there is one significantly larger change in the whole history, it will not make all the other cubes barely visible. However we also find it important to base the alpha value on the whole history to get a better idea if at some time there were bigger changes. We determined that an alpha that is $2/3$ based on local maximum and $1/3$ based on global maximum works well in our case. We cannot generalize this decision, but rather suggest to calculate alpha based on both local and global maximums.

Changes. 2D Meta Information

As can be seen on Figure 5.3, our visualization also contains cyan and yellow spheres. They are situated in 2-dimensional planes and contain additional information about packages and rules for each version. Cyan spheres reside in a rule-version plane and each of them represents changes made to the rule in the version. Yellow spheres are related to the changes in packages and reside in package-version plane. To better explain the location of the spheres, we provide an illustration in Figure 5.4. We use a different shape: spheres, as they represent completely different data from cubes. We also color them with distinct colors that are different from the critiques delta color codes.

The cyan plane is located on the side of the matrix. It is in front of the matrix if you are looking from the position where the versions increase from left to right. We find this to be a common position for inspecting the matrix, as in western culture people expect time to travel to the right. We place the spheres in front of the visualization as changes in rules are not frequent and most of the time we want to correlate exceptional changes of critiques with the changes of rules.

Packages have significantly more changes in comparison with rules, in fact each version is an update of some packages. We found

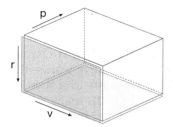

Figure 5.4: Meta planes illustration.

that the change metadata can obstruct the rest of visualization. This is why the yellow plane is located at the bottom of the matrix, as it is common to look at 3D visualizations from above the horizon level.

The crosshair extends slightly beyond the change planes making it easy to see if a sphere is on the same line with a square. Hovering over spheres also displays the crosshair in the same way it works with cubes. This allows a user to easily see what cubes are related to a change, what other changes happened in the same version, or in which versions the same rule (package) was changed.

The change spheres can be used in two ways. One of them is to easily see if there was a change in the rules or packages for some set of squares. For example in Figure 5.3 a cursor is hovered over a cube that is on one line with the other ones and the crosshair is penetrating a cyan sphere ③ revealing that the rule of the hovered cube has changed in this version. Secondly one can start by looking at the patterns in changes ① ② and inspect the impact that they made based on the visualization.

Visual Features

The visualization provides many different pieces of information, as we have a cube position based on 3 coordinates, color, translucency and 2 extra planes that have a sphere position based on 2 coordinates. It may seem that this amount of data pollutes the visualization and makes it hard to understand. For this reason we identify 2 sequential questions that a user of our visualization wants to answer.

1. What are the irregularities in the system's evolution?

2. Why did this irregularity occur?

To answer the first question a user can use the camera movement and identify clusters of cubes. We based our approach on the proximity principle: a pre-attentive feature that allows us to cluster closely-situated visual elements in a fraction of a second [Ware 2004]. The principle works in 2D space so that the 3D visualization is eventually projected on a plane. We took into account many aspects, such as the sparse nature of the critique deltas and translucency of smaller deltas, to avoid occlusion, because it can cause false clusters to appear on a 2D projection. The cube clusters form lines, as seen in Figure 5.7. At this phase spheres do not obstruct the visualization; the color of cubes is not as important as whether the cubes are there or not, and whether the proximity is preserved during the camera movement.

After a user has identified the pattern of cubes and locked on it, the second question should be answered. In this case the rest of the visualization comes into play and helps a user to understand what is the version, which rules have changed in this version, were the critiques added or removed, *etc.*

Interaction

The visualization supports orbiting of the camera around the 3D matrix with a mouse. Also a keyboard can be used to move horizontally or vertically the point at which the camera is looking (the same one used as the center of orbital movement). By hovering with a mouse over visual elements user can see a popup (⑤ in Figure 5.3) with an information about the version, rule and package of the element. Also a crosshair appears on the hovered element and spans the whole matrix including planes with spheres. This allows a user to easily identify which elements are on the same line. For example on Figure 5.3 the crosshair's line is passing through many red cubes and a cyan sphere. This demonstrates that all the critique changes are on the same line, and are reported by a rule that has changed in this version ③. Another line of the crosshair is penetrating a yellow sphere, which means that the package related to the hovered cube has changed in this version ④.

While we rely on the natural clustering, we also provide slicing functionality that allows a user to hide the unneeded parts of the visualization to avoid being distracted by them. These options are accessible from the context menu of any cube. One kind of slicing removes all cubes that are more than two steps away from the selected one. This can be done based on all three dimensions: by versions, rules or packages. As a result only a slice with a thickness of 5 cubes is visible as shown on Figure 5.9. The other kind of slicing simply generates a 2-dimensional incidence matrix visualization (Figure 5.10). This slicing approach eliminates the distortion caused by perspective, but also lacks information about the neighbor slices.

We encode a large amount of data into the visualization, but some information like a textual change log summarizing the patch cannot be conveyed by colors or layouts. For this purpose we provide a dialog window with a textual description of the patch release notes together with links to the discussions on an issue tracker.

Finally we envision our visualization as a tool for identifying and removing anomalies. For this purpose we provide an option to log an anomaly which can be:

- rule anomaly: all critiques with a certain rule and version;

- package anomaly: all critiques with a certain package and version;

- version anomaly: all critiques with a certain version.

After being logged the cubes related to the anomaly will be removed from the visualization to simplify the detection of other anomalies. This action can be accessed either from a cube's context menu, of from the dialog window with a patch summary.

5.1.4 Case Study

Figure 5.5 displays our visualization applied on the full Pharo data set described in subsection 5.1.1. In this section we will do a step-by-step walkthrough for decomposing the evolution, and provide the obtained results.

Decomposing the Data Set

To find anomalies in the system's evolution we orbited around the visualization and looked for patterns that stood out. All the

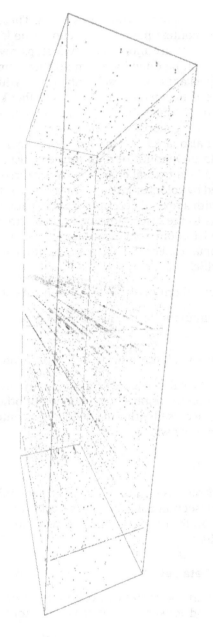

Figure 5.5: A complete visualization of Pharo critiques over the history of 680 incremental patches.

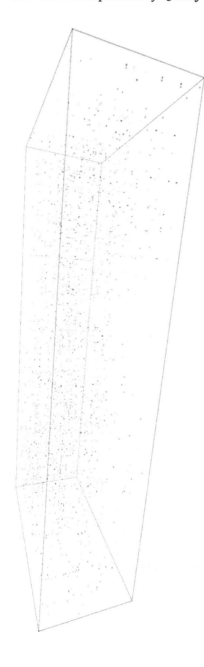

Figure 5.6: The complete visualization of Pharo critiques after the cleaning of anomalies.

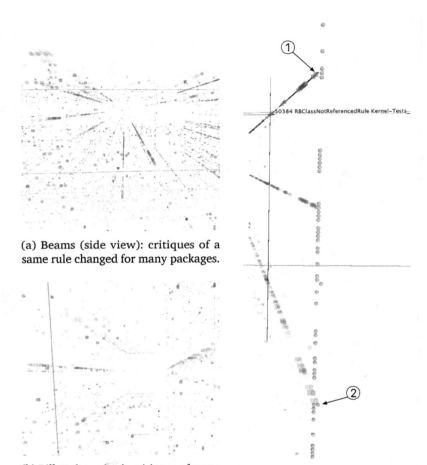

(a) Beams (side view): critiques of a same rule changed for many packages.

(b) Pillars (top view): critiques of many rules changed for a same package.

Figure 5.7: Common critique anomalies.

50384 RBClassNotReferencedRule Kernel-Tests_

Figure 5.8: Core rule refactoring. ① tip of the crosshair not penetrating a cyan sphere. ② follow-up anomaly.

patterns that we identified by this approach had a line made out of cubes as their base component. The cubes that make these lines represent critiques from the same version. There are two types of this lines: *beams* – the critiques are related to a single rule and form a horizontal line (Figure 5.7a) and *pillars* – the vertical counterpart where the critiques are about a single package (Figure 5.7b).

A few patterns especially attracted our attention. The critiques in this case form a *wall* of cubes by spanning both multiple rules and packages (Figure 5.9). All anomalies of this kind were related to critical issues in the system that were immediately fixed. This is why all the walls came in pairs of opposite colors separated by at most one version. For these anomalies slicing the visualization to present only a subset of cubes in a range of 5 versions was useful to remove all the noise around and investigate the pair of walls alone. The two dimensional representation shown on Figure 5.10 helped us to isolate one plane even more and remove the perspective distortion. We viewed the patch comments for each version and analyzed changes made. After this we saved the version numbers together with comments about the reason of each anomaly. In the end we hid the walls to remove unneeded obstructions.

The second kind of special pattern that drew our attention appeared in cyan spheres and was related to rule changes. There were two versions where changes occurred in almost every rule, which is most likely a sign of refactoring, as many similar components of a working system have changed simultaneously. One of them did not have any beams, and the other one is shown on Figure 5.8. The visualization contains 4 beams. The crosshair on one of them does not penetrate any sphere from the cyan pillar ①. This allows us to easily see that the beam is not aligned with the pillar which means that they are from different versions. The only red beam ② is also not in the version with rule refactoring, but it follows a blue beam and also has a cyan sphere on its end. The next hypothesis can be formed by simply looking at the visualization: "There was a refactoring globally performed on all the rules, because of which two rules were broken and one of them was fixed in the following patch." By looking at the patch summary we confirmed that our hypothesis was correct except for the detail that one of the rules was not broken but rather fixed during the refactoring session. This also

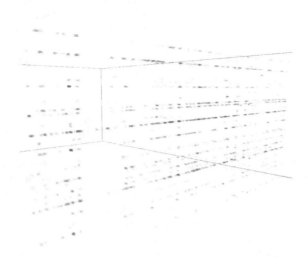

Figure 5.9: "Wall": Critiques of a significant amount of rules changed for many packages.

Figure 5.10: 2D representation of one version.

explains why it did not receive any more attention in comparison with other rule that was immediately fixed.

After dealing with walls and rule refactoring we started to process other beams, as they were more prominent in comparison with pillars. The standard workflow went as follows:

1. **visually locate**: we visually explored our visualization and focused on the lines that can be seen at Figure 5.7a. We used camera movement to change the angle of view and viewpoint to ensure that the cubes are not forming a line only in one projection.

2. **analyze relations**: we used a crosshair as demonstrated in Figure 5.8 to better understand how are the other elements situated relatively to the beam. We also used slicing to focus only on the critiques of a few versions (Figure 5.9), or on the critiques of a single rule by using 2-dimensional slice similar to the one in Figure 5.10. The slicing functionality was used to identify if there were other beams in the same version or in the whole history but related to the same rule.

3. **understand the cause**: at this point we mainly relied on the patch summaries, issue tracker messages and source code diffs to understand the reason of changes and the cause of the anomaly.

4. **log and hide**: we annotated the anomaly with the explanation about the changes that caused it. Finally we hid the anomaly to avoid distractions during further explorations.

After dealing with beams we moved to pillars. We quickly noticed that most of them are related to the changes that were introduced in the package that they represented. It is debatable whether there is a benefit of logging and removing such kind of anomalies from the data set. They are related to one of the main questions of software's quality analysis: "how does this change impact the software quality?" However, we decided to log these anomalies anyway, as we wanted to investigate if there are other causes and also by removing or hiding them we could reveal other less prominent anomalies. The strategy for processing pillars was the same one as for processing beams. We naturally finished our analysis when we

Type	Subtype	Number
Complete versions		6
Rules (32)	added or removed	8
	fixed or broken	17
	other (non-related to rule changes)	7
Packages (45)	added or removed	42
	modified	3

Table 5.1: Number of recorded anomalies by type.

were not able to detect anomalies any more. Figure 5.6 depicts the final state of the main visualization without the anomalies that we identified during the cleaning process.

Obtained Results

The quantitative results of the decomposition that we performed are presented in Table 5.1. The minority of anomalies affected both many rules and packages of a version. This is natural, as such anomalies are related to severe issues in the system. In our case there were six such cases that formed three pairs, as each defective patch was instantly fixed or reverted. Only one such pair was related to changes in the quality validation system. It was very hard to identify the cause of all such anomalies, and this involved reading patch summaries, bug tracker issues and even code that was changed.

For most of the logged anomalies critiques of many rules affected a single package. Out of a total of 45 anomalies, 42 were related to the packages being added or removed. This could in fact be easily detected automatically. The remaining three anomalies were caused also by package-related changes, where a significant amount of code was changed in one patch.

The third type of anomaly – critiques about a single package that originated from many rules, had 32 occurrences. Eight of them were related to an addition or a removal of the rule. This subtype of anomaly could be detected automatically. 17 anomalies were related to the rules being fixed or broken. And the smallest subtype with only seven cases is related to the anomalies that are not related to the rule changes. Some of them were results of a planned eradication of the critiques of a certain rule. The others were related to the specific changes of the source code that had an impact only on a single rule.

Despite eliminating all the visual anomalies, we missed a few cases where a single cube had a large delta of critiques. For example the average delta is around ten critiques and two cubes had a delta of more than 2 000 critiques. These cases are very rare and very hard to detect, as in the 3D matrix they are represented by a lonely completely opaque cube that is not very different from its surroundings. On the other hand these anomalies can be easily detected by sorting all deltas by their absolute value and inspecting the largest ones.

The most important findings were concluded from the anomalies related to the critiques of a whole version, critiques related to rules that were not caused by the rule changes and critiques of a single rule that affected only a single package in a version. These findings show weak points in the system, and the integration approach. Rule-related anomalies caused by the rule changes allowed us to understand how requirements to the code quality were changing over time.

Anatomy of the Anomalies

Most of the **package-related** anomalies were caused by addition or removal of the packages themselves. These changes were caused by replacing old submodules by new alternatives, integration of new features or removal of the unused ones. The smaller amount of anomalies caused by dramatic package changes happened in the packages that belong to external submodules. They are versioned separately from the main project and the integrated versions contain more changes.

Rule-related anomalies have a more diverse nature. Poor value of the critiques reported by rules was the main reason for their removal. The rules that were added captured the design decisions of different parts of the project. Some of them were related to a method invocation order, others provided suggestions about the usage of core API migrations, or about the methods that have to be defined under certain circumstances. Rule fixes either were focused on capturing the violations that were missed or excluding false positives from the results. Also few rules had their scope reduced to avoid the overlap of critiques. The regressions in rule functionality happened because of two reasons: either a mistake was made during a refactoring or the precision of a rule was sacrificed in favor of performance. After analyzing the data set and rule anomalies in particular we can suggest stakeholders a test that can warn about these kinds of changes in rules prior to integration.

Some rule-related anomalies were caused by changes in the code. For example one of them reported many invocations of undefined methods. This was caused by the changes to the API of an icon factory. Another case involved the deprecation of a widely used API, which caused many deprecation warning critiques. A third case involved the addition of support classes that reported a high number of "unused class" critiques. The last two cases were negated by counter-anomalies where issues introduced previously were fixed. We suggest the stakeholders to review the quality validation in their integration process, because according to our findings the critiques that can be easily solved with a simple automatic refactoring were ignored and the criticized code was integrated.

Wall anomalies are the most interesting type. We identified three pairs of them and only one was related to the changes in the quality validation framework. It occurred when the server-side validation system was broken, and the changes made were intended to fix the issue. As a result integrated changes broke the validation system completely and were instantly reverted. Other two anomalies were caused by integration of a changes with invalid source code. Beside breaking the quality validation the changes also caused issues with source code recompilation and were fixed in the following versions. We encourage stakeholders to investigate the integration process, as two changes that broke the validation were nevertheless integrated. We also advise to add a test of source code integrity to detect similar issues more easily.

Finally, our case study contained two **single-cube anomalies** that were related to a single issue. The rule violated by these anomaly is checking whether a class contains methods identical to the ones defined in traits [Schärli et al. 2002] that the class is using. The first anomaly was caused by a package rename refactoring during which all trait methods were copied into the classes of that package. The second anomaly appeared 170 versions later when the duplicated methods were removed. The issue was identified because developers noticed the related critiques. However we advise the stakeholders to investigate why these changes were integrated in the first place, and solve the duplication bug of rename package refactoring.

5.1.5 Discussion

In this section we reflect on our use case experience and discuss both positive and negative aspects of the visualization.

The visualization represents anomalies as natural clusters of data that are easily detectable by visual exploration. The orbital camera movement was essential to identifying whether the detected pattern is not an accidental alignment of the elements in the current projection. For the same reason we suggest to use the same size for all the cubes, as different sizes will complicate the perception of dimensional positioning. The sparse nature of the data is also very important for the visualization. Because the changes to the critiques should not be frequent and large, most cubes are highly translucent or completely transparent and do not obstruct the view of the ones positioned behind them.

The movement interactions were not very user-friendly and could benefit from improvements. For example visual elements could be selectable, after which they will serve as a center of the orbital movement. Also the effort spent on getting closer to a desired element to inspect it can be enhanced by using semantic zooming [Woodruff et al. 1998]. As the visualization presents data in an immersive 3-dimensional environment and mainly relies on pre-attentive processing possibilities of a human brain we believe that it can be interesting for researchers who explore visualizations in virtual reality [Merino et al. 2017].

Slicing was another important feature. It allowed us to isolate an interesting piece of information from the rest of the visualization that was obstructing the view. We found out that 3-dimensional slicing (Figure 5.9) was the most useful when applied to the version axis. This allowed us to see the changes in the adjacent versions and often we were able to detect cases where some changes were rolled back, or continued on other entities. The same kind of slicing was useful for the packages axis, however this is related to the nature of our data set. As mentioned previously the packages form implicit groups that have same base name and different suffixes. These groups usually change together, so having a 5 block deep slice allowed us to capture up to 5 co-changing packages. This was not always practical as sometimes more than 5 packages formed a group. This suggests that we need to have support for variable slice depth. 3-dimensional slicing was not applicable to rules, as every rule evolves independently of the others. The main goal of slicing the rule axis is to see if there were similar anomalies for the rules throughout the whole history. If the slice contains more than 1 rule, the anomalies from other rules will also appear in the slice and make the analysis more complex. Thus 2-dimensional slicing (Figure 5.10) worked the best for the rule axis. Similarly 2-dimensional slicing was useful in every case where a single relation between two properties (rule, package or version) had to be examined. Also the possibility of creating a multiple slices can be useful when inspecting similar changes separated by a large period of time.

While obtaining the information about an inspected patch, the main summary and issue tracker discussions were not always enough. Sometimes we had to analyze which classes and methods were changed in the particular patch. Additionally it may be useful to have support for calculating the difference between non-adjacent versions, this can help in detecting rollbacks. We detected a few anomalies that were related to each other in our case study. This requires not only a possibility of multiple slices or selection, but also some features to record this relation between anomalies.

A unique feature of our visualization was the metadata representation by spheres. We found the information about the rule changes extremely useful. It allowed us to easily identify if there were changes made to the rule related to a visual element, and see if it was also changed in the nearby version. Similarly we could see if the other rules changed in the same version. In some cases changes to the rules were driving our exploration because we were able to detect patterns of cyan spheres.

On the other hand, information about the package changes was not very useful. Because of the nature of our data set changes to the package are frequent, and yellow spheres obstruct the view if placed on top. We placed them at the bottom and then it was hard

(a) Co-changing packages.   (b) Spheres at the bottom of pillars.

Figure 5.11: Package change metadata.

to see how they are related to the data. There were some situations where yellow spheres clearly revealed groups of packages that changed together (Figure 5.11a). Also during the pillar inspection yellow spheres at the bottom of pillars were clearly identifying that the critiques are related to a historical group of package changes (Figure 5.11b).

The difference between the usability of cyan and yellow spheres can be explained by the nature of our problem. The yellow spheres represent the changes of packages. These changes are the the building blocks of software evolution. They are frequent and we consider their existence to be natural. Rules also evolve, but at a much slower pace and they do not clutter the view. Our main focus is to identify the changes in rules, because they are not as common to us as the changes in packages. These relations can be different in another use case that will focus on something other than changes in rules and packages. This is why we encourage the users of our approach to experiment with positioning the meta information planes on the different sides of the visualization.

We already mentioned in subsubsection 5.1.4 that many of the anomalies were related to the addition or removal of rules and packages. Before decomposing the visualization into the anomalies we were not expecting such a high percentage of them to be caused by addition or removal. Now we can recommend the users of our approach to automatically detect and remove the anomalies from the visualization based on this criterion. Also we suspect that some of the other anomalies can be detected by a statistical approach, or at least be shortlisted statistically. We have not investigated this idea, but without building the visualization we did not know what our data looks like and what the statistical approaches should look for.

We presented a scenario where quality critiques were influenced by the changes of both quality rules and source code. We believe that this visualization can be applicable to many problems where one value depends on the other two co-evolving values. The immediate related problems that can be tackled by the approach concern failing tests and changes in the performance.

Many visualizations suffer from scalability issues, as the visual elements become too small and the encoded metrics cannot be read. In contrast, our approach relies on the significant amount of data that allows a user to detect anomalies that span the whole visualization. We expect that at some point the number of visual elements will decrease the performance of visualization, but this can be mitigated with a sliding time window approach [Zimmermann and Weißgerber 2004]. Also at some point the lines that form anomalies may become too thin to identify them. In this case we suggest to group the entities into blocks that unite the entities with some feature but evolve independently of each other. For example in our case packages can be grouped by their base name, while rules can be grouped by their category.

5.1.6 Conclusions

We have presented an approach for visualizing the evolution of a value that depends on two co-evolution properties. The main goal of the approach is to detect, identify and log the anomalies that prevent the evolutionary analysis of dependent values. The visualization is constructed in 3-dimensional space and relies on the sparse nature of analyzed data. It enables quick detection of the anomalies with the help of pre-attentive cluster recognition and provides multiple visual features that enable a user to obtain more detailed information. While many visualizations try to provide meaningful information in each visual element, our approach can be referred to as an *anti-matrix*, because the data provided by the matrix serves secondary purposes while we focus on detection of *structures* in the 3D space that indicate anomalies. This makes our approach resistant to large dataset sizes *e.g.,* we don't analyze individual cells of a 200x100 matrix, but detect walls, pillars and beams that can consist of different number of elements.

We evaluated our approach by analyzing quality evolution of a real project measuring 520 thousand lines of code. The quality was affected by both changes in the source code and changes in the rules that define quality concerns. We were able to successfully identify most of the anomalies, while the remaining ones can be easily detected by using statistical approaches. We analyzed 85 anomalies and categorized them into different types. Some of the types turned out to be easily detectable automatically while the summary about the others can help to deal with the anomalies in similar problems.

We described all the possible scenarios that can be followed with our visualization, but one can also benefit by using it for a single task such as: 1. obtaining a general overview of the system to understand the status of anomalies; 2. extracting anomalies caused by only one of the co-evolving parameters; 3. completely cleaning the system of anomalies. Also our approach can be combined with others to perform a more advanced analysis.

5.2 QualityAssistant Impact on the Rules

While using the visualization from section 5.1 we discovered 25 changes to the quality rules of Pharo that changed behavior of the rules. It is also worth mentioning that in the development cycle of Pharo 5, over 60 quality rule-related bug reports, feature requests and enhancement suggestions were opened which is twice as many as the average in previous years. These values quantify the impact that QualityAssistant had on the Pharo ecosystem, but do not tell anything about the changes in detail. As the rule modifications were initiated by Pharo developers, we believe that the in-depth analysis of the changes can help us to better understand the needs of the developers and categorize the rules from different perspective.

In this section we summarize the changes introduced to the rules after QualityAssistant was integrated into the Pharo IDE and demonstrate how promotion of a quality analysis tool together with a feedback loop can help in shaping the quality rules themselves. We also analyze 3 rules that were removed from the system and 15 new rules integrated into Pharo or related projects. The relationships between them show that developers prefer rules that are easy to understand and capture important violations to those that express general programming practices.

5.2.1 Changes to the Rules

According to our investigations the changes to the rules after QualityAssistant was integrated can be naturally divided into three categories: bug fixes and usability improvements, removal of the rules or a part of their functionality, and creation of new rules. In this section we describe the most interesting use cases in each category.

Bug Fixes and Usability Improvements

QualityAssistant greatly increased the number of critiques that Pharo developers encounter during programming sessions. This provoked complaints and bug reports about the critiques that provide false information. For example, one rule checked whether the category of a method is the same as the category of the overridden method from a superclass. However it also detected cases where a method has a category while the overridden method is uncategorized. In other words the rule suggested to remove the criticized method from its category to match the status of the overridden method, which is nonsense and contradicts another rule that checks whether all methods are categorized.

Some bugs had more severe consequences. For example a rule named "*Modifies collection while iterating over it*" modified abstract syntax trees during source code validation. This is completely unexpected and unacceptable behavior as the validation process destroyed parts of the system, much like a virus. The bug was detected only after the integration of QualityAssistant. Some developers noticed a strange behavior of the methods that were inspected while the live static analysis was active. As the bug was in a SmallLint rule — it also potentially affected all methods validated by CriticBrowser. The bug was not detected before although the rule is not new. This suggests that CriticBrowser was sporadically used despite a quarter of developers claiming to use it on a daily basis according to the survey in subsection 4.1.1.

Another group of rule changes is related to usability improvements. Most of them are caused by the inability of a rule to explain a violation. For example the rule for detecting usage of a "*soon-to-be deprecated API*" detected a method, but did not specify which part exactly violates the rule. Another rule suggests replacing `detect:ifNone:` with `anySatisfy:`, but also reports a critique if `contains:` is used. This happens because at some point the rule's functionality was updated, but its description was left unchanged. While many usability problems were caused by poorly developed rules, there were some issues related to a completely wrong design of a rule. For example, one rule detected whether an abstract class has references. While a developer gets a feedback about the class, the exact piece of code that references it is unknown. This issue was resolved by shifting validation from detecting abstract classes that are referenced to detecting methods that reference an abstract class and highlighting the source code where the abstract class is accessed.

In some cases we went even further than just enhancing the explanations of critiques. For example one rule detected a class that has all subclasses with the same-signature methods, but does not itself define an abstract method with that signature. The rule did not specify which method is missing in the class. Not only did we add the method name to the critique explanation, but also we created an action that automatically creates the required abstract method. Automated resolutions of critiques contribute to the usability of the rules by making them clearly actionable, as well as offering better explanations.

In total over the course of development of Pharo 5 around 20 integration requests were related to improvements in functionality or usability of quality rules. All the changed rules were present in Pharo prior to the QualityAssistant integration and no one of the developers mentioned their deficiencies. This is why we claim that live static analysis reports together with a well-organized feedback loop are essential to keep quality rules in a good shape.

Rule Removals

During the evolution of Pharo 5, three quality rules were completely removed. All of them had the same properties, namely they brought attention to common beginner mistakes, but were annoying to experienced developers. Additionally we allowed developers to react to the critiques by sending positive or negative feedback. The critiques of all these rules received a large amount of negative feedback. Next we provide the description of each use case.

The most hated rule checked whether a yourself message is present at the end of a message cascade. We describe the rule in more detail in Appendix A. The rule is very important if a person does not know how a cascade works, because one may expect to obtain the receiver of a cascade as a result while a cascade actually returns the result of the last message. If a developer is aware of this, there is little benefit in being reminded that there is a cascade without a yourself message at the end. There are many cases where this message is not necessary. Moreover, one may want to actually obtain the result of the last message in the cascade instead of the receiver. In this case yourself has to be omitted on purpose.

The second rule detected whether the messages like ifTrue: have a block as their argument. This is another useful rule for beginners that annoys experienced developers. None of the users of Pharo 5 found it useful, and the rule reported critiques only about special cases that worked well without blocks. For example:

```
size = 1 ifTrue: ':' ifFalse: 's:'
```

is a perfectly valid piece of code that is easier to read compared to the version with blocks, and executes faster as there is no need to unwind block contents.

The last rule detected methods that reference an abstract class. This rule was previously modified and so is also described in the previous subsection. In essence the rule raises the programmer's awareness of possible instantiations of an abstract class which can lead to a potential invocation of an abstract method. However this also includes the usage of utility methods on the class-side. Moreover abstract classes often provide factory methods [Gamma et al. 1995] that return their subclasses. For example `UIManager default` will return an instance of a concrete `UIManager` subclass that is the default for the current setup. It is also not possible to only focus on the `new` messages that are sent to the abstract classes, for example `String new` creates an instance of a concrete `ByteString` class which is a subclass of an abstract `String` class.

In all cases the probability of a critique being an actual issue was much lower than the negative impact that the issue would cause if it was present. However all the rules from this subsection had an educational emphasis which means that they may be useful for a teaching configuration of the system.

Rule Addition

As developers became more aware of the critiques in their code, new rules were introduced to inform developers about the violations. Most of the rules were requested by the Pharo community or the developers of different frameworks and we ourselves implemented many of them. Originally all the rules were packaged together with the SmallLint engine. We tried to put each new rule in the same package that contains the code related to that rule. For example if a rule describes how a testing framework should be used, we package it with that framework: this way if someone uses the framework he or she will also get critiques from the dedicated rules.

Only a few rules were placed in the SmallLint package. Two of them are rules related to Pharo core functionality. One of them suggests to use `ifNil:` and `ifEmpty:` instead of `ifNilDo:` and `ifEmptyDo:` as they will be deprecated soon. Another one suggests to replace `Smalltalk at:` with `Smalltalk globals at:`, because of changes in the core API. The other group of rules captures new architectural constraints of SmallLint rule classes and so was packaged in the SmallLint package.

All the other rules are packaged together with their related projects. For example a rule that warns about a usage of special `BoxedFloat64` and `SmallFloat64` classes was shipped with the Kernel package. Another rule that suggests to use `assert: a equals: b` instead of `assert: a = b` was added to the SUnit package. First of all this enhances modularity of the system: one can simply unload the SUnit package and load another testing framework. In this case the SUnit-specific rules will be uninstalled together with the package. Additionally this packaging strategy encourages the maintainers of the package to also maintain the rules that are related to their code.

Rules were introduced to three projects that are being developed in parallel with Pharo and have their own repositories. Two of these projects, Rubric and Roassal [Bergel 2016], required rules to check the order of method invocations. Both projects make use of builder pattern [Gamma et al. 1995] where the order in which the builder methods are invoked impacts the final result. For this purpose a special type of rule was introduced that allowed developers to easily specify the required order.

Rules for the third project, *Glamorous Toolkit*[*], were different by their nature. One of the rules detects classes that have extension methods coming from the toolkit but do not define special methods that are used to show examples about these classes. Other rules relate to performance issues that could arise during the definition of the extensions. In particular computation of the values can be delayed by passing expressions wrapped in blocks and allowing a builder to lazily evaluate the block as late as possible.

When we conducted interviews with QualityAssistant users in section 4.4 the developers mentioned that some rules from external frameworks like *Glamorous Toolkit*, were particularly useful because they acted as a just-in-time documentation. As we discovered in this section, these rules addition was motivated by QualityAssistant.

---

[*]`http://gtoolkit.org`

The 15 new rules can be grouped into five distinct categories based on their nature, impact of their critiques, and ways to resolve them.

Migration rules describe a transformation from one API to another and can automatically rewrite code. For example usage of `ifNil:` instead of `ifNilDo:`. If violations of these rules are ignored, in the future the code may fail because of the removal of the old API.

Private access rules warn about usage of functionalities that are not meant for public access. For example `SmallFloat64` is a system-specific class that is present to ensure good performance of floating point calculations on 64-bit systems, but it should not be used directly in the code. Violations of these rules can be ignored only under very special circumstances, such as deliberate low-level programming, but this may lead to unexpected errors, non-portable code, or even issues in the future as a private functionality evolves more frequently.

Invocation order rules detect if the order of message sends makes sense. For example if the `edges:` message is sent to a graph builder before the `nodes:` method is used to specify nodes, the edges will not be initialized. If critiques of these rules are ignored the desired result will not be obtained.

Class structure rules capture design guidelines that should be followed while subclassing or extending classes. They check whether certain methods are overridden, or that particular methods are present if certain conditions are met. The rule that checks if the `hash` method is overridden together with the "`=`" method belongs to this category. If left unchanged the violations will either result in an unexpected functionality, or cause a rejection of integration as the project's design guidelines are not followed.

Lazy evaluation rules in our case were represented by a single pair of rules in Glamorous Toolkit. They detect expressions that could be evaluated lazily to exploit the design of Glamorous Toolkit. Violations of these rules will result in poor performance and will complicate exception handling, if left unchanged.

All of the added rules target exact violations such as a wrong API usage, violation of design conventions or inefficient code. The violations are related to the project where the rules belong rather than some general OOP practices. Moreover, most of the violations will certainly result in defects and so cannot be ignored.

Another important aspect worth mentioning is the implementation of the rules based on their type. Migration rules can be easily expressed with the refactoring browser [Roberts et al. 1997] rewrite engine. For example use of the old SUnit API can be easily detected with the expression:

```
self should: [ ``@object ]
```

and changed to the new API with:

```
self assert: ``@object
```

Private access rules can simply detect access to entities with a certain annotations, which is implemented in many languages through access modifiers. To specify invocation order a special DSL like *usage contracts* [Lozano et al. 2015] can be used. Class structure can be easily checked by directly manipulating class objects *i.e.,* by obtaining a list of methods defined in a class, and validating whether they adhere to certain requirements. To support lazy evaluation rules we worked with raw AST nodes: we identified builder message nodes that should receive blocks as arguments and verified whether the argument nodes are literals or blocks. If the arguments are represented by other kinds of expression nodes we generate a critique. We believe that there is no single approach or DSL to define quality rules but rather many different ones that target a certain type of violation and provide a different level of actionability.

Structural Changes

The introduction of QualityAssistant triggered some minor structural changes in SmallLint rules. Some duplicated functionality was removed from certain rules. For example one rule checked whether = 0 is used instead of isZero and =nil is used instead of `isNil`. But another rule also included the latter case and additionally checked if `~= nil` is used instead of `notNil`. Duplication became easy to detect by shifting the critiques from the rule-centric view in the CriticBrowser to an entity-centric view in the QualityAssistant. For example, previously a developer was using a browser that displayed violations per each rule making it complicated to notice among many critiques that the same violation is reported by two rules. On the other hand, if a developer browses a method that contains `= nil`, critiques from both rules inform that `isNil` should be used instead, making the duplication evident.

Some rules were split into multiple ones to allow for better filtering or due to performance decisions. For example, a rule that checks whether a sent message is not implemented was split into two: a fast one that checks whether a message sent to self or super is not implemented in the hierarchy, and a slow one detecting whether a method with the selector of a message is implemented anywhere in the system. This way the slow rule may be excluded from the live feedback of QualityAssistant to avoid lengthy delays during development process, while the fast rule will still detect a subset of critiques.

5.2.2 Conclusions

We have introduced a set of intrusive plugins called QualityAssistant into the IDE used by Pharo developers. The plugins educated developers about the the existence of quality rules and issues in their code. At the same time QualityAssistant started a feedback loop that triggered many changes to SmallLint rules.

The analysis of the changes made after integration of QualityAssistant shows that many important bugs in rules were detected and fixed. Unproductive or annoying rules were removed, while new helpful rules were added. The analysis of the added and removed rules helps us to identify the features that are important for developers in the rules, namely:

1. clear explanation of a critique that exposes the source of violation;

2. suggestion of a solution or automated resolution of an issue;

3. high impact of the critique *i.e.,* critiques that detect guaranteed bugs are valued more than the ones that warn about hypothetical problems.

Moreover the new rules introduced into the system capture domain-specific properties of the projects that they represent. This suggests two distinct types of rules:

Internal rules are specific to a team, company or community and focus more on the general questions. These rules may define style, focus on common metrics like number of methods in a class or describe an architecture of a project. Their value comes from capturing agreements that are already present in the community. To change them one has to negotiate the change of the principles in the community.

External rules come together with a library or framework and act as documentation. This type of rule supports migration to a new version of API and detects improper or inefficient usage of a library. The value of these rules comes from automatically providing crucial information about possible bugs and their solutions as early as possible. Maintainers of projects should be in charge of changing the related rules similarly to how documentation is changed.

5.3   The Quality Evolution Roundup

At the beginning of this chapter we set a goal to analyze the quality evolution of Pharo 5 and explore whether the integration of Quality-Assistant caused any changes. As a side effect we created a novel 3D visualization to decompose the quality fluctuations that happened due to the changes in the rules. Then, as another side effect we obtained the rules changes that caused anomalies in the quality evolution. By analyzing the changes that happened to the rules, we could understand the requirements of the developers, and improve the architecture of rules to cope better with the future tasks.

After cleaning the critiques dataset from the anomalies we could not find traces of any impact caused by the QualityAssistant integration on the trend of the Pharo's quality evolution. By analyzing the situation more carefully we realized that this result has a meaningful explanation. The versions that we used to form our data set are "incremental updates" that are validated by a CI server and peer reviewed by Pharo developers including someone of the small core development team. From this perspective QualityAssistant does not ensure the good quality of code, but rather reduces the time that developers need to submit a good quality patch, and reduces the time needed to perform a review. In fact, the novice developers whom we interviewed in section 4.4 confirmed that by using QualityAssistant they learn about best code quality practices, while the core Pharo developers said that QualityAssistant draws their attention to suspicious pieces of code and guides their code reviews.

Needless to say, we cannot assess QualityAssistant based on the quality evolution mined from the Pharo 5 incremental updates. On the other hand, during the analysis we discovered the rule changes that can be also seen as a validation of QualityAssistant, because its integration motivated developers to add new helpful rules or improve the existing ones. Based on this finding we want to emphasize the importance of the adaptability of the static analysis framework. From a certain version of Pharo, the developers received a powerful tool QualityAssistant that kept them continuously informed about the quality of their code. However, the information that the tool provided was not always correct and this reduced the usefulness of the tool. Thankfully, the developers were able to modify the analysis system to suit their practices better and eliminate the incorrect data. There is a good chance that the developers would have abandoned the tool if they could not modify it.

6 | Quality Assistance in Other Tools

Most of this dissertation is focused on QualityAssistant— a small list of static analysis critiques situated under the main code editor of Pharo. We used QualityAssistant as our primary test vehicle because it is integrated in the Nautilus code browser — the tool that Pharo developers use the most to read and write code. As a result we ensured as much interaction of software developers with static analysis as possible. However, programmers also use other tools specialized for various software development contexts. In this chapter we show the feasibility of static analysis integration for other tools. We exemplify how static analysis feedback can benefit from run-time information, relaxed time constraints, and various UI features of software development tools. In section 6.1 we describe the updates to the tools already available in Pharo. In section 6.2 we present a visual approach to design inspection that is facilitated by static analysis data and is designed to solve the problems of modern code review.

All the tools presented in this chapter use static analysis information provided by the Renraku model that we described in chapter 3. The model provides a convenient way to obtain critiques about a code entity and thus frees the tool developer from the burden of setting up a static analyzer and running it. The critiques are modeled as full-fledged objects that encapsulate all the details about the issue that they represent. They also provide actions that help to better understand and resolve the violation. As a result the main concerns of a tool developer are filtering of the available critiques (based on

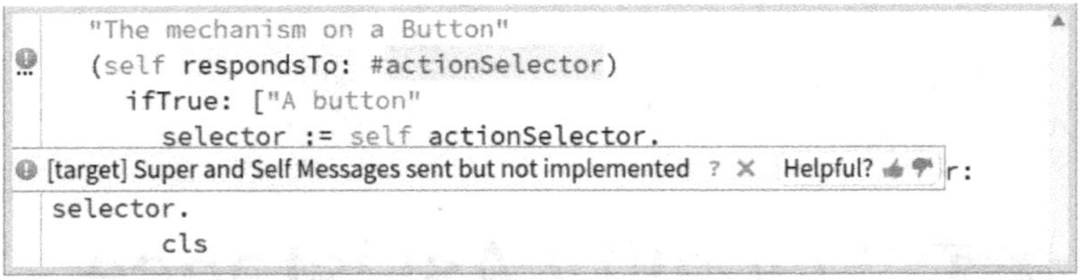

```
    "The mechanism on a Button"
    (self respondsTo: #actionSelector)
        ifTrue: ["A button"
            selector := self actionSelector.
```
[target] Super and Self Messages sent but not implemented ? ✕ Helpful? 👍 👎 r:
```
    selector.
            cls
```

Figure 6.1: Critiques highlighted in the source code.

the selected entity or rule) and the representation of them as user interface elements. Finally, the extensibility of Renraku played an important role in prototyping custom analysis. This chapter serves as a validation for Renraku.

6.1   Common Pharo Development Tools

6.1.1   Message Browser and Inline Critiques

Based on the QualityAssistant survey from section 4.2 we identified that many developers do not know about the possibility to highlight a piece of code that violates a certain rule. Without this feature it can be complicated for a developer to determine the source of a critique. Additionally, some developers that we interviewed (in section 4.4) disliked the design of QualityAssistant because it uses too much of a precious space of their code editor. To mitigate these deficiencies we decided to experiment with an inline design that is commonly used in other IDEs. As shown in Figure 6.1 critiques are presented to a developer by highlighting the respective source code intervals and placing an interactive icon on the window's side bar. The icon can be used to view the description of the critique and perform actions.

This feature was first integrated into Message Browser — a tool used to browse methods that either implement a selector, send a message with that selector, or satisfy some other kind of query. Then the inline critiques were moved to the Nautilus code browser as an alternative option for the default QualityAssistant list at the bottom of the window. Some developers prefer the original QualityAssistant UI because they can easily see the names of critiques without having to hover over the sidebar, or they can passively ignore the critique list all together. On the other hand there are developers who prefer to have inline critiques, and switched to this option as soon as it became available. It is natural for humans to have their own opinion and preferences, but we want to explicitly highlight the fact that in both cases the developers are happy with the live feedback.

6.1.2 CriticBrowser

Originally CriticBrowser was based on the old SmallLint implementation and the move to Renraku brought a few benefits. Figure 6.2 shows the CritiqueBrowser suggesting a fix to a missing method critique. SmallLint could not suggest such fixes before, because it could only transform methods and was not able to perform a more complicated refactoring like a method addition. Thus in the original CritiqueBrowser a user would see only a message *"Method defined in all subclasses, but not in superclass"* and the definition of the class where the method is missing without any suggestion which exact method is missing. This example demonstrates how advanced critiques improve all the tools that use Renraku. Additionally, the implementation of CriticBrowser was simplified. In the original implementation, the tool had to possess an extensive knowledge about various kinds of rules. If a critique belonged to an architectural rule, CriticBrowser would provide a way to open a dependency analyzer; for a transformation rule — perform the rewrite. Once CriticBrowser was moved to Renraku, it relied on property actions and thus all the domain knowledge remained in the critiques themselves.

6.1.3 Calypso

In Pharo 7 the Nautilus code browser is expected to be replaced by a new one called Calypso.[*] This is a very crucial event for QualityAssistant for survivability reasons. A few years ago the Usage Contracts project [Lozano et al. 2015] brought a live static analysis plugin into the contemporary code browser in Pharo. Later the code browser was replaced by Nautilus, and as the developers of Usage Contracts did not have time to re-implement the plugin, the live

---

[*]https://github.com/dionisiydk/Calypso

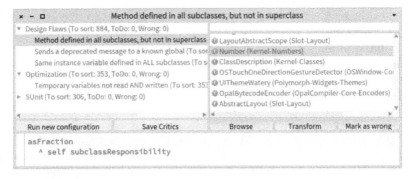

Figure 6.2: Critique browser suggests a solution to a critique.

feedback was lost. In our case, the developer of Calypso personally added the live quality feedback into the code browser.

The majority of Smalltalk code browsers have a notion of a method protocols — groups that do not impact functionality and are used to categorize methods. Calypso brings a concept of dynamic protocols that, instead of just relying on a method category, can dynamically group accessors, inherited methods, methods that come from a trait, *etc.* The author of Calypso created a dynamic group for Renraku critiques. The list of protocols with the critiques group can be seen in Figure 6.3 in the third column from the left. The subgroups are taken from the rule groups, and allow developers to easily browse all the methods that have for example optimization critiques about them.

The integration of static analysis into Calypso also exemplifies the idea that the original tool developers should be the ones who integrate static analysis into development tools. Renraku enables this by providing a convenient way to obtain the static analysis information without having to learn how an analyzer works. Additionally, Renraku acts as a interface on top of multiple analyzers and thus a developer does not have to decide which analysis to integrate and maintain.

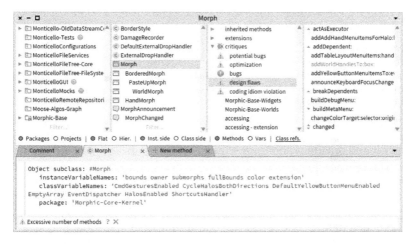

Figure 6.3: The Calypso browser with a critique method group.

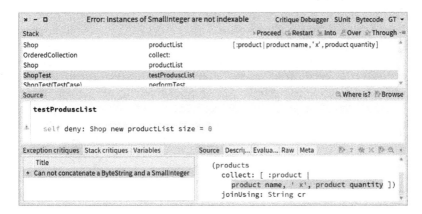

Figure 6.4: The Pharo debugger augmented with static analysis information.

6.1.4 Debugger and Stack Critiques

Probably the second most widely used tool to write code in Pharo is the debugger. It is a common practice to run some code, get an exception, open a debugger, edit the code in the debugger, and continue execution. After the success of QualityAssistant some developers asked us to augment the Pharo debugger with static analysis feedback. We used the inline critiques approach that we mention previously, to integrate the static analysis feedback into the debugger's code editor. While inline critiques are not special in the context of a debugger, we realized that there is much more information available during a debugging session. For example we could obtain critiques for all the methods from the top of the execution stack and try to suggest the source of the bug based on hot spots. Additionally, the information about the variable types that is present in a debugger and can be used to perform a more detailed analysis. Figure 6.4 depicts a debugger opened on the *"instances of X are not indexable"* exception. This exception occurred because a non-collection object was passed as a parameter to a concatenation method while the method expects an indexable object. On a higher level a developer just tried to concatenate a string with a number, but the reason for the exception is hidden below multiple layers of the string concatenation implementation. This is a common mistake, which can be easily solved by converting a number to a string. At the bottom left of the debugger window we added a list of critiques identified by the execution stack analysis. The single list entry reports the concatenation of a string with a number, shows the exact location of the issue in an area on the right, and can even automatically refactor the code to perform the number to string transformation.

The stack critiques are not yet available to Pharo developers, and we are still investigating which kind of mistakes can be detected this way and what is the best way to communicate these critiques to the developer.

6.2 Quality-Driven Code Review

Besides augmenting Pharo development tools with static analysis reports, we analyzed the issues of modern code review techniques and to which extent they are addressed by the available code review tools. Then we created a completely new tool, empowered by static analysis, to demonstrate our approach of visual design inspection.

The most common form of code review is *peer review* — a semi-structured approach that can be more easily adopted (and adapted) for the specific needs of development teams [Cohen et al. 2006a]. During peer review, the changes to source code are reviewed by a small number of developers just before being integrated.

Modern code review is supported by dedicated tools. Popular examples include Gerrit and Rietveld by Google, Code Flow by Microsoft, Phabricator by Facebook, Crucible by Atlassian, *etc.* Most tools provide a set of common core features, such as a diff view of the changes to be reviewed, the ability to comment parts of code, discuss changes, and mark a code patch as reviewed.

Ideally, a code review is an efficient way to improve code quality, detect critical bugs, and share code ownership [Rigby and Bird 2013]. This effectiveness motivated a study of developer expectations and encountered difficulties during a code review [Bacchelli and Bird 2013]. The authors found that the main reason to perform a code review is to find defects in code and to improve the code written by others. The main difficulty of reviewing code is in understanding the reason of a change that one has to review. As a side effect of this problem, reviewers start to focus on the easier to detect code style problems, in essence going for the low hanging fruits. A natural consequence of this is that reviewers are not able to effectively tackle software defects, and the ultimate goal of improving code quality is hindered.

We conducted a critical analysis of the state of the art of code review tools and analyzed the features that they provide [Tymchuk et al. 2015a]. Then we compared the most common features of the available tools with the shortcomings identified by related research.

We propose an approach called Visual Design Inspection (ViDI) which uses visualization techniques to drive the quality assessment of the reviewed system, exploiting data obtained through static code analysis. ViDI enables intuitive and easy defect fixing, personalized annotations, and review session recording. To demonstrate and assess the approach we implemented a running prototype as an open source MIT-licensed tool with the same name.* We provide

---

detailed showcase scenarios that illustrate the benefits and potential of ViDI and our vision. The showcase scenarios also clarify and exemplify the actual shortcomings that need further investigation and research.

6.2.1 The Visual Design Inspector

Philosophy and Core Concepts

As we saw in the previous section, most review tools focus on a specific context, the one of pieces of code (patches) that need to be reviewed before being allowed into the release version of the system code base. We argue that this is a specific scenario of a wider context, namely the one of continuous assessment of the quality of a software system. We believe there is the need for an approach where quality concerns are not reported only for patches, but become an integral part of the development process. In the ideal case such a quality control would be performed in real-time, but for the time being we opt for a session-based approach, where developers verify the quality of parts of a system (either old parts, or newly contributed parts, such as patches) in dedicated quality assessment sessions. ViDI is thus rooted in the concept of a *review session*, which can focus on a package or a set of packages. During the review session, all changes made by reviewer are recorded and can be accessed in the future. The system to be reviewed is presented in a dedicated visual environment augmented with automatically generated quality reports. The environment is self-contained: The reviewer can navigate, inspect and change the system from inside ViDI: ViDI supports both system understanding and improvement in an integrated environment. As a system can be changed during the review session, ViDI automatically re-evaluates the quality assessment, to keep the reviewer updated about the current state of the system. Sessions can be stopped, and the session-related data can be archived for further usage. Furthermore, the session can be visually *inspected* at any time to understand the impact of the review, in terms of the amount of changes and how the system under review improved from the perspective of code and design quality.

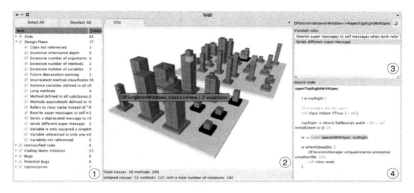

Figure 6.5: ViDI main window, composed of ① quality rules pane; ② system overview pane; ③ critiques of the selected entity; ④ source code of selected entity.

User Interface

The main window of ViDI is depicted on Figure 6.5. It consists of three horizontal panes, which respectively provide i) a list of categorized quality rules violations (critiques), ii) an overview of the system, and iii) detailed information about a selected entity.

Critiques List. This pane provides an organized overview of the occurrences of critiques in the system. The list of critiques provides two columns containing the name of the rule and the number of critiques occurrences in the current system. Rules are hierarchically organized into predefined categories. Each rule and category can be deselected with a checkbox next to it. This removes the critiques related to this rule (or category) from the other panes of the tool. By default, all categories are selected.

The **System overview** consists of a city-based code visualization [Wettel 2010]. We depict classes as bases on which their methods are stacked forming together a visual representation of a building. A status bar provides a short summary about the system, containing information about the classes and methods under review, those which have critiques, and the total number of critiques on the system. The system overview pane supports immediate understanding of the quality of the system under review, relating its structure and organization with how critiques are distributed over it. In this view, method and class colors also depend on the amount of critiques. The element with the most critiques is colored in bright red. This color gradually changes to gray as number of related critiques decreases. Elements with no critiques are colored in gray. The view considers only the critiques and categories selected in the critiques list. Hovering over the elements of the city displays a popup with the name of the element and the number of critiques, if present. Clicking on an element selects it: When an element is selected, it is colored in cyan and can be inspected in the rightmost pane of ViDI.

The **Selection Pane** is dedicated to inspection and modification of an entity (*i.e.,* package, class or method) selected in the system overview. The name of the selected entity is displayed on top of the pane, while the rest of the pane is split in two parts. In the top half, the pane contains the list of all visible critiques about this element. Selecting one of the critiques highlights the problematic parts in the source code, which is displayed in the bottom part of the pane. The reviewer can make changes in the source code and save them. When an element is changed, the critiques are re-evaluated.

ViDI employs Renraku actions to provide automatic fixes. This option can be triggered from the context menu of a critique. For example, Figure 6.6 shows how by clicking "Perform transformation" in the context menu ViDI will automatically fix the problematic part of the method.

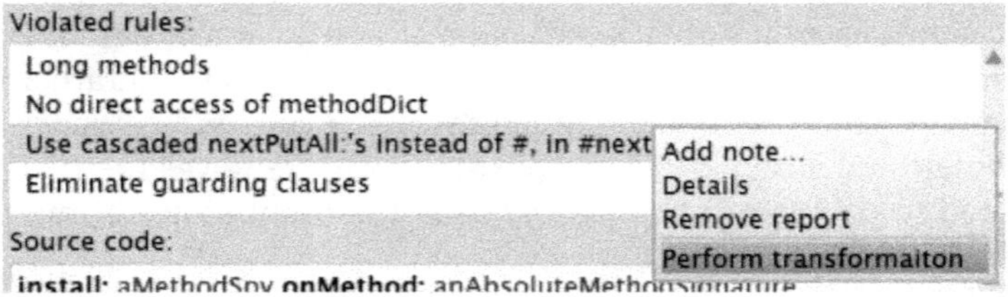

Figure 6.6: Automatically fixing a critique.

Another option offered by the context menu is the inspection of the details of a critique that illustrate its rationale and further details. Finally, another option is to add a note, the purpose of which is for the reviewer to leave a comment related to the specific critique, propose a solution, or details on its rationale. Figure 6.7 shows a specific example of this scenario.

Figure 6.7: Adding a note in ViDI.

After a note is added, it is displayed in the list of critiques: Such a note is essentially a custom critique by the reviewer. Notes have the same role and importance as critiques: They are stored alongside entity critiques and they are equally considered fundamental for the purpose of evaluating the quality of a system. The purpose is to elevate reviewer comments to the same level of automatically generated critiques.

At the end of a session, or at any moment, the reviewer can reflect on the session itself and understand the effects of the review on the system. We designed and implemented two complementary views: the critiques evolution view (Figure 6.8a), and the changes impact view (Figure 6.8b).

The **Critiques evolution view** displays how the amount of critiques changes in time during a review. Figure 6.8a shows an example where the graph is monotonically decreasing, with minor exceptions (around 17:36). With this view, the reviewer can visualize the fact that the session decreased a significant number of issues in the reviewed code, from 119 initial critiques to 26 critiques, in a timespan of around 35 minutes. The visualization also displays the impact of each change, displayed as dark semitransparent circles, whose radii correspond to the change impact.

The **Change impact view** shows a histogram of changes made during the session to reason on the number of changed code that corresponds to the number of resolved critiques. The x axis contains the sequence of changes in the code, the y axis shows the *change impact*, a simple metric of how the change impacted the reviewed code. As a preliminary metric we chose the number of changed characters in the source code. We plan to study alternatives that

145

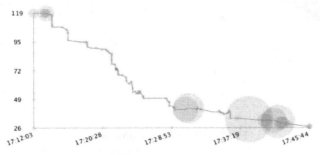

(a) Critiques evolution during a review session.

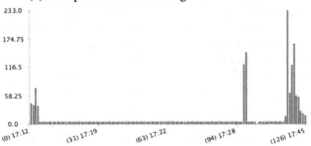

(b) Impact of changes made during a review session.

Figure 6.8: Reviewing a Review Session.

would take into account the nature of each change to code, like refactoring choices. In both views, hovering over an entity shows a popup with information about the change, while clicking on it opens a dedicated diff view of a change.

6.2.2   ViDI Demonstration

In this subsection we walk through two review sessions to demonstrate ViDI: The former is about ViDI on ViDI itself, and the latter is on DFlow[*] [Minelli et al. 2014], a profiler for developer's actions in the IDE).

---

[*]http://dflow.inf.usi.ch

ViDI on ViDI

We developed ViDI following the principle of *dogfooding* [Harrison 2006], that is, by using ViDI on ViDI itself to continuously validate its capabilities. Once we reached a working prototype status, we started reviewing and developing ViDI with the support of ViDI itself. This allowed us to refine concepts and ideas, but it also helped us to upkeep the quality of ViDI's code, which is what we focus on here. At the moment, ViDI contains 23 classes with 201 methods and extends 14 classes with 33 methods. Figure 6.8a and Figure 6.8b, that we discussed previously, show one of the many review sessions of ViDI. That session involved mainly method categorization. Such critiques are Smalltalk specific: In Smalltalk, methods can be categorized, meaning that a developer can assign it a category representing the class of purpose of the method. ViDI helped to solve these critiques, and others that were automatically fixable, many times during its own development. This ability is effective to focus on more important design issues, alleviating the burden of checking a long report originated by a static analysis tool. Moreover, by assigning an impact to changes, we could also more effectively review the more important changes we performed on ViDI. Figure 6.8b shows how most of the changes are in fact minor, automatically resolvable, issues of low impact. The changes with higher impact focus on three different moments of the session, in the beginning and in the end of a session, when the developer solved a number of style-related critiques involving the use of conditionals, and other functional critiques that required refactoring of methods. Unfortunately, a couple of rules solved at the end of the session suggested invalid changes to the code, and led to malfunctions of ViDI that were corrected in subsequent reviewing sessions. This suggests that SmallLint, the static code analysis technique that we currently use, has some shortcomings; in the long term, we plan to address them specifically, but at the current point, we assume that the critiques we obtain can be generally trusted. Finally, the developer noticed some missing features from ViDI while reviewing a specific piece of code. In particular, he added two accessors to get the start and end time of a session. Even if the modification was not motivated by solving a critique, this is an interesting use case of ViDI that we plan to better support, for example by asking the reviewer a motivation for the change when it is not clear which was the issue he was trying to solve.

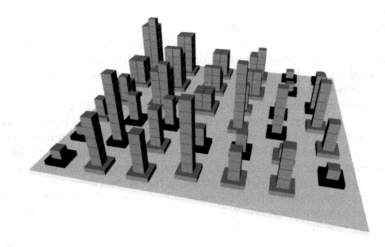

Figure 6.9: Vidi quality status.

The current quality state of ViDI can be seen in Figure 6.9; it still contains few critiques that we could not resolve. As we are working with Pharo, a dynamically typed language with no type inference [Palsberg and Schwartzbach 1991], many rules are based on limited imprecise heuristics. This leads to misleading false positives. For example, since ViDI uses reflection, we found rules that identified bad style in references to abstract classes, which however is fine when using reflection methods.

This suggests either refinement of SmallLint critiques or, more likely, improvements of ViDI to manage exceptions and the personalization and localization of rules.

Another class of rules that we needed to ignore are rules that are general and conceptually fuzzy, like rules detecting overlong methods. For example, some specific API usages (*e.g.,* for visualization) tend to generate methods which contain many parameters to be set through method calls. This domain-specific API usage generates relatively long methods, which in turn generate critiques by SmallLint. However, such critiques are false positives because such long methods are due to domain-specific usages, and not because

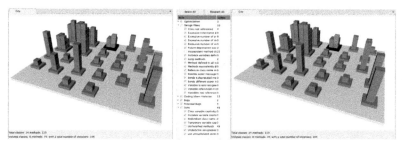

(a) All critiques visible.   (b) Unclassified and inconsistently classified methods critiques hidden.

Figure 6.10: Initial state of the review sessions.

of method complexity. Again, this suggests the need for a specific management of exceptions.

ViDI on DFlow

DFlow consists of 8 packages, 176 classes and 1,987 methods. We reviewed a single package which consists of 23 classes and 119 methods. The package uses *meta programming* [Bouraqadi et al. 1998] to instrument and augment the Pharo IDE with additional functionalities. The quality of such a package is essential, as it can break the IDE and cause issues to development itself.

The starting point of the session is depicted in Figure 6.10a. The system overview pane shows a relatively distributed number of critiques. The two categories with the largest number of critiques are *"Unclassified methods"* and *"Inconsistent method classification"*. Critiques point out that a method has no category, or that the category of the method is different from the one of the method that it overrides. As these violations are related to documentation, and they do not lead to real bugs, we can decide to omit them by deselecting the checkboxes next to related rules. The resulting view gives us a clearer image to focus to more serious issues (Figure 6.10b). Another way to assess the quality of the system is to deselect all rules and then select just one or a few them. This allows to focus on specific kinds of issues that may be more important to a project.

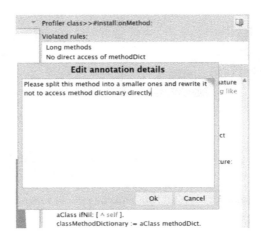

Figure 6.11: Commenting on complex issue.

After filtering unimportant rules, a reviewer can automatically resolve issues related to code style and optimization. This leaves more complex issues that neither can be dismissed because they are important, nor can they be fixed automatically. For example there is a method violating two rules: the method is too long and it directly accesses a class method structure, which is specific to the current implementation of Pharo.

Suppose the reviewer is not the author of the method. The fact that critiques cannot be automatically fixed leaves the reviewer in front of a choice: He could either manually fix the method or leave a note for future inspection. In the latter case, the reviewer can ask the author to split the method and remove direct access to the internal class as shown in Figure 6.11. The note is left as a full-fledged critique in the system that can be inspected when reviewing the system. Notes are stored in ViDI and can be manually exported and imported by a reviewer.

Figure 6.12 shows the critique evolution of the session, which was rather dramatic: the number of critiques went from 105 to 11 in just ten minutes. At the beginning, critiques almost instantly dropped under the mark of 58 critiques. This was caused by the automated resolution of categorization issues. Then, after *20:29* mark style and optimization issues were fixed which generated

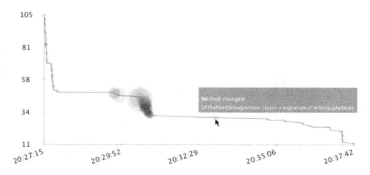

Figure 6.12: Critiques evolution on a DFlow review session.

changes in the code, and so this part contains dark circles with larger diameters. These fixes also correspond to a steep drop in the number of critiques, because resolution was automated. The next change appears after *20:32:29*.

By hovering over the circle, the reviewer can see a popup which informs that this change was a modification of a method called `signaturesForDebugActions` in a class `DFProfilerDebugAction`. A diff of this change can be seen by clicking on the circle. This was a non-trivial issue that could not be automatically fixed, as the reviewer was understanding how he should resolve the issue. There is also a longer period without any change after the resolution in `signaturesForDebugActions`. This is because the reviewer was trying to understand how to resolve the second issue and writing a note to the author. At the end there is a part where the critiques line descends. These changes corresponded to the reviewer manually categorizing methods. Finally, close to the end, another steep drop can be seen. This happened because the reviewer categorized methods on the top of a class hierarchy and overriding methods at the bottom were categorized automatically.

6.2.3 Discussion

As we illustrated in subsection 6.2.2, ViDI can be used not only to visually inspect the design of a software system, but also to effectively solve critiques, ranging from simple style checks to more complex issues. The case studies we analyzed pointed out both benefits and important shortcomings of ViDI that we now analyze to take a critical stance against our tool.

Critique Representation and Detection. We found relevant shortcomings in the way SmallLint critiques are represented and detected. There is significant research to be done in detecting high-level design issues, for example by integrating mechanisms based on object-oriented metrics [Lanza and Marinescu 2006]. Another shortcoming we found involves false positives, like the ones related to long methods. While some rules require improvement in their representation, others may require a new representation of rules themselves. All SmallLint critiques return a boolean result about the evaluated code entity, that is, they either violate the rule or not. This is too rough: Ideally, rules should have a severity grade [Lungu 2009], to identify the entities where rules are violated more seriously and to focus on them first.

Fixing Critiques. In the current state, some critiques can be solved automatically, while others require manual fixing by the developer. Requiring a manual fix does not mean that we should not provide at least semi-automatic support for resolution, especially for critiques that would require specific refactoring methods. For example, proposed changes can be presented to the reviewer before being applied, and can be personalized to adapt them to meet the reviewer intention.

Notes and Review support. ViDI gives a basic support to leave notes on code entities, which are treated as full-fledged critiques. This idea can be expanded in many directions, for example to support more complex comments [Brühlmann 2008; Hao et al. 2013] that are common on other code review tools, or to provide dedicated mechanisms to handle exceptions and personalizations.

Diff support. We provide basic support for code diff. ViDI should be improved by considering related approaches outside the area of code reviewing. For example, the approach of supporting integration of source code changes provided by Torch [Gómez et al. 2010] could inspire solutions for ViDI on code contributions, and not on the analysis of entire systems.

6.2.4 Conclusions

We presented ViDI, an approach that envisions quality inspection as the core concern of code review. We focused on this particular concern after a detailed analysis of the state of the art of code review approaches, which is another contribution of this dissertation. ViDI supports design inspection by providing a dedicated user interface that enables an immediate understanding of the overall quality of a system. It leverages automatic static analysis to identify so-called critiques in the code, and it enables their inspection and fixing, either manually or automatically. Moreover, we designed ViDI to record reviewing sessions that can be inspected (and reviewed) at any time, highlighting how the system has been improved during the session, and enabling a quick evaluation of the impact of changes performed by the reviewer. We performed a preliminary assessment of ViDI by providing two case studies, involving the review of ViDI on ViDI itself and on DFlow — an advanced IDE profiler.

From the engineering point of view ViDI is significantly more complicated than the tools that we presented before. Most of those tools were either displaying all the critiques about a single entity (as in QualityAssistant) or all the critiques produced by a single rule (as in CriticBrowser). On the other hand ViDI had to summarize critique information based on a single rule, a rule group or an entity, dynamically toggle visibility of the critiques and provide a detailed and actionable information per software entity. Renraku played an important role during the development of ViDI and served as the core meta model. Renraku provided rich critiques and ViDI just had to filter them and display in the UI elements according to the setup made by a user. Additionally, Renraku critiques already maintained references to the related rules and targets making it easy to track what should be re-validated after source code changes take place. Finally, ViDI relied on the extensibility of Renraku to add user notes as an addition to the critiques.

 # Conclusions

In this thesis we presented our vision of quality-aware tools. We based our quality criteria on static analysis algorithms. To combat the fact that software developers do not use static analysis tools, we integrated the quality analysis into the development tools that programmers use in their daily routine. We studied the acceptance of the quality feedback integration, its impact on software developers, and feasibility of such tools in general. As a result, we ended up with many satisfied developers, a few tools that developers are actively using, a couple of prototypes that yielded important experience, and finally a unified code quality model. In this chapter we summarize our main contributions and chart a road map for the future research in quality-aware tooling.

7.1 Contributions

7.1.1 Live Quality Assistance

We augmented the main Pharo code editor with live static analysis feedback known as QualityAssistant. The live feedback co-exists with an on-demand batch-mode static analyzer CriticBrowser which is not systematically used according to our survey. To assess QualityAssistant we performed an initial usability survey a couple of weeks after its integration and a series of interviews almost one year later. Both the survey and the interviews showed that most of the developers find live feedback of QualityAssistant to be useful.

The closer examination of the interview responses showed that the intrusiveness of QualityAssistant is one of its most important features because the developers see critiques as they program and can quickly resolve the reported issues. At the same time, the narrow scope of QualityAssistant's critiques is related to the development context of the developer and simplifies comprehension of the reported issue. Improved critique understanding in turn helps to fight false-positive reports that are not an exception to the static analysis of QualityAssistant. We discovered that developers can learn about best development practices and API guidelines from static analyzers. Domain specific rules provided by third party libraries were especially useful for our interviewers, as these rules helped developers to better understand how a library should be used and how to avoid trivial mistakes.

Besides human assessment of QualityAssistant we also analyzed changes that happened to the quality rules after the static analysis integration. While there were many rule-related bugs fixes, some of the rules were completely removed and new ones were added. We discovered that the removed rules had a high false-positive ratio and thus annoyed most of the developers in the live-feedback setup. On the other hand, Pharo developers added new rules to communicate API changes, design contracts, and optimization suggestions with the help of QualityAssistant's intrusive feedback.

Currently QualityAssistant is integrated into the main Pharo distribution and provides two opportunities. First of all, other researchers can introduce their own analysis and benefit from the existing live feedback infrastructure while evaluating their approach. Secondly, the main developer of QualityAssistant is also the author of this dissertation who is not going to maintain the live feedback framework anymore. Thus the future evolution, stagnation, or deterioration of QualityAssistant can act as yet another evaluation of how important is the live quality feedback for the Pharo community.

7.1.2 3D Decomposition

We encountered a challenge while analyzing the evolution of code critiques in the development versions of Pharo 5. Changes in critiques for each patch were influenced not only by the changes in source code, but also by the changes of quality rules. To investigate the problem, we visualized the critiques in a three-dimensional space, where axes were represented by the incremental versions (time), quality rules, and source code packages. Such visualization allowed us to easily identify anomalies caused by changes in rules, changes in code, and failures of the validation system. Critiques related to the anomalies formed distinct shapes that resembled walls, pillars, and beams in a building. We believe that this approach is applicable to other datasets, where one value depends on two other independently evolving variables.

7.1.3 Unified Quality Model

We devised a single static analysis model that can be reused in various analyzers and development tools. The Renraku model is based on three key concept: a rule that can validate code, a critique which is reported by a rule, and a target of the criticism. Renraku follows two goals: to simplify integration of available analyzers into new tools, and to simplify addition of new analyzers to the existing tools. Thus the approach targets two groups of people: analysis developers and tool developers.

We used Renraku to augment eight development tools with static analysis feedback. These tools operated in various contexts such as code editing, code inspection, debugging, and code review. The UIs of the tools allowed various levels of customizability, from minimalistic inlining in a message browser to custom debugger plugins or even a dedicated visualization in ViDI. In all the cases we found that a short text and a small icon is enough to communicate basic information about a critique with a user, while more sophisticated interaction can be achieved through custom actions. Each action can have short description and an icon as well, and an arbitrary code that will execute upon activation. The references to rules and targets allowed the tool developers to group critiques in the tools that operated on large scopes of code and required sophisticated categorization.

While working on quality rules we identified a few actions that were common for many critiques. These actions are *viewing the rationale, banning the critique,* and *suggesting a solution* to the detected problem. In a few special cases rule developers added their own actions that open special tools such as a dependency browser.

Two developer implemented their own custom analyzers on top of Renraku. One analyzer reports issue tracker entries related to a source code target while the other one assists a developer to achieve a good test coverage and automatically validates whether all test pass for a source code entity. The developers of both analyzers had little to no knowledge of how to develop extensions for the code editor, but as they only had to work with the quality model. As a result they managed to accomplish integration of each analyzer in about 10 hours which is a relatively short time for such task.

7.1.4 Visual Design Inspection

Apart from augmenting the existing development tools with quality feedback, we studied the shortcomings of the modern code review, devised a quality-driven Visual Design Inspection approach, and built a prototype tool to demonstrate it. The approach consist of

identification of problematic parts of a software system based on a visualization enhanced by static analysis reports;

inspection of the faulty software and the related reports, resolution or documentation of the issue;

review of the session in terms of the changes to the source code and variations in the quality.

We demonstrated how the ViDI approach can be applied to improve quality of the ViDI tool and another software project.

7.2 Quality-Aware Tooling Recipe

Based on our experience of augmenting software development tools with static analysis feedback, we would suggest the following recipe for those who want to increase the quality awareness of software developers:

1. *Integrate static analysis into the most commonly used development tools.* If you are an IDE developer, or if all the developers in

your community use the same tool, live feedback can give you an edge in sharing the quality guidelines. However, if the developers use various IDEs it can be easier to focus on a tool where the development effort converges in one place such as a CI server. Do not stop at a single tool, as each of them targets software development from a different angle.

2. *Ensure the consistency of the quality guidelines.* It would be inappropriate if a developer had to follow one set of rules while developing software and another upon the integration. Of course, certain rules can be less appropriate in the context of certain tools, but the core guidelines have to be shared across all the tools. A single quality model used by both analyzing and development tools can simplify the implementation if the analysis is performed by multiple analyzers and has to be displayed in multiple development tools.

3. *Enable community tailoring of quality rules.* It is common to introduce quality assistance with generic rules, but they will not fit all the possible projects and workflows. After some time the users of quality assistance will want to modify or remove some rules, and add the ones that are specific to their use cases. Unless it is very easy for a casual developer to modify the rule base (which, to our knowledge, is currently an unsolved problem), you should assist your users to change the rules.

4. *Favor discussion and consensus over majority voting.* Not all the proposals regarding the changes that should be made to the rules will be unanimous. It is better to discuss the conflicting opinions, as often they indicate misunderstanding of some design principles and may negatively impact the development experience of certain groups of developers.

7.3 Future Vision

7.3.1 Quality Modeling

Questions from this category target the features of Renraku and tackle the conceptual issues of external properties.

Advanced Routing in Renraku

At the moment Renraku acts as a layer between tools and analyzers that allows tools to easily obtain external properties about any target generated by available analyzers. The analyzers can be easily added of removed, but the obtained external properties come from all the analyzers currently loaded into the system. During the interview in section 4.4 we learned that developers may prefer to see the critiques of certain rules in a specific tools instead of everywhere where is it possible. We believe that this is more important in terms of analyzers. Thus Renraku has to implement more of a "routing" logic. We envision a functionality that delivers (or routes) the external properties from an analyzer A to the tool T, where T explicitly subscribed to the information that originates from A.

Another issue to keep in mind is that at the moment Renraku does not provide any optimization against re-computation. For example if five browsers are opened on the same method and it is updated, all the browsers will ask for new critiques, and these are going to be re-computed five times. So far this did not cause big problems for us, but the re-computation issue will become more and more prominent in the future when more tools and analyzers will rely on Renraku. Maybe this should be solved with caching, or maybe there is another approach based on subscriptions, scheduling and notifications that can be explored as a part of the *routing model*. For example, Renraku could react an update in source code, check if there are any subscribed tools that are currently active on the changed piece of code, run the required analyzers once and notify the tools about the result of the analysis.

More Analyzers in Renraku

At the moment most of Renraku's use cases are based on a single analyzer: SmallLint static analysis rules. Lately, other kind of analyzers have started to appear such as the issue tracker linker, or the backend that ensures that code is thoroughly tested. These analyzers, however, are still in their infancy, and we expect that, as they mature, there are going to be some requirements that Renraku cannot fulfill. For example the increased number of analyzers will increase the average number of the reported properties which will complicate the comprehension of the reports. It is important to study the requirements of analyzers and evolve Renraku accordingly because in the context of quality-aware tooling, static analysis is not the only source of information about the software quality.

More Property-Based Tools

One of the Renraku's key ideas is the concept of an external property: an actionable object which encodes a piece of knowledge about a code entity. Besides various critiques, there can be completely different types of properties, such as an issue tracker entry. At the moment most of these uncommon properties were demonstrated in the context of QualityAssistant which has a simplistic user interface. Although the more sophisticated tools such as CriticBrowser and ViDI rely on the Renraku model, they operate strictly on static analysis critiques. As quality-aware tools should be aware about the various aspects of quality, one has to investigate to which extent tools can rely on multiple sources and what are the shortcomings.

In theory, CriticBrowser is a tool for browsing automatically collected external properties about source code. At the moment the properties are static analysis critiques, hence the name: CriticBrowser. In case these properties are bindings to an issue tracker the tool would turn into an issue tracker browser or a local issue tracker client. We expect that in practice it is more complicated to build a client for an issue tracker, and the possibilities and limitations of such a tool should be researched in more detail in the future.

Object critiques

In subsection 6.1.4 we demonstrated how one can benefit from the critiques of objects other than source code entities. In the example we analyzed an execution stack to identify a commonly known mistake and suggest an automated solution for it. This motivates a new powerful assistance framework especially for dynamically typed languages. When we perform our analysis on a static source code we lack a lot of information about the variable types, but if we are in the middle of a debugging session, all the information from that execution point is available to us and to our tools. Besides analyzing the execution stack, a debugger could validate available objects against their domain rules to potentially detect a malformed object that will help to localize a bug. At the moment we do not know whether there are enough use cases that follow the described scenario and whether object-based rules will not require more time and resources in comparison with static typing.

7.3.2 Human-Critique Interaction

In this subsection we focus on the questions that revolve around the interaction of a developer with code violations. Most of the questions listed here arose during the analysis of QualityAssistant.

Critiques on various levels

In section 4.4 we learned that there is no single best place to report quality violations to a developer. A solution to this would be to have multiple tools based on the same quality model (such as Renraku), and have a possibility to easily define which tools should use a certain rule. This solution requires a user study to identify how developers would use this setup. Based on our experience we would suggest to have quality feedback in at least three development stages: 1) live feedback in a code editor; 2) pre-commit validation of the new changes; 3) pre-integration validation on a CI server.

QualityAssistant Usage

In this dissertation we evaluated QualityAssistant from the user perspective by conducting surveys and interviews, as well as from the software ecosystem perspective by analyzing changes caused by the QualityAssistant integration. Based on the evaluation results we can say that the live quality feedback is important and beneficial for software developers. The next logical question to address is *"how do developers use QualityAssistant?"* The live quality feedback overlaps with the main activity of a software developer, and thus fine tuning of the feedback system can have a reasonable impact in the development experience. As a starting point, we recorded developer interactions with QualityAssistant and published them online [Tymchuk 2017b]. The data was used to motivate a related research in software refactoring, but the analysis of QualityAssistant usage in fine detail remains future work.

Rule Creation

Related research made a strong emphasis on the importance of domain specific rules. We have confirmed this in section 4.4 as some of the interviewed developers identified that they learned important concepts of frameworks that they used from custom rules provided by the frameworks. Additionally, in chapter 5 we analyzed the rules that were updated to meet the latest requirements of Pharo developers.

At the same moment, most of the rules are created by dedicated developers or very curious individuals. In our case, the rules were created by us, by Pharo developers, who were previously implementing quality rules, and by a few developers who asked us to teach them how to develop rules. We believe that the status of static code analysis would radically change when after having an idea about a new rule an average developer would personally implement it. This is a broad question and we see a little interest towards it because the current research of static analysis focuses on the correctness, execution speed, and feasibility of quality rules while the developer-friendliness is rarely taken into account.

Other Ecosystems

All our work was based on Pharo, which gave us significant benefits such as the reflective capabilities of the programming language and a single IDE used by all the developers. We are interested to learn if the results of our experiments can be replicated on other languages and IDEs. We do not see a technical issue why it should not be possible, especially when there are tools such as IntelliJ IDEA which comes with a live static analysis. We suppose that there could be "cultural" issues, because programmers who use certain technologies may have different visions on how programming is done. Finally to replicate our change in the development ecosystem, one has to maintain a certain user base. An interesting candidate for this would be a company like Microsoft, which provides a complete development stack with the C# programming language, the Visual Studio IDE, and the Team Foundation Server with CI capabilities. Another interesting candidate is the SonarSource company who became popular with their CI for code quality validation called SonarQube [Campbell and Papapetrou 2013]. Now they start to provide live feedback with the new SonarLint tool. Obviously, the idea of SonarSource is to have the same validation happening both live and on the CI server. The only question is whether they will promote a single platform to implement quality rules and port the existing ones, or they will focus on their own small set of rules. So far the company has followed the latter strategy.

7.4 Summary

Static analysis is a mystical concept that has been proven to be useful and not used at the same time. We boldly stated that static analysis has to be an integral part of software development tools and to prove our point, we augmented tools from the Pharo development ecosystem with static analysis reports. As a result we obtained plenty of positive feedback both from surveys that we organized and informal discussions with developers. More importantly however, we changed the *status quo* of static analysis in Pharo. Nowadays Pharo developers casually discuss static analysis rules, wonder why there is no quality assistance in a certain tool that they use, and ensure that the new tools come with static analysis support.

We created a unified quality model as a side-effect of augmenting Pharo development tools with static analysis. The model is used to separate the concerns of code analyzers that produce critiques from the tools that display critiques in their UI. As it became possible to add custom analyzers, developers started to experiment with their own analysis that went beyond standard code pattern checkers. In a way developers showed that software quality can be also validated by unit tests, its deficiencies are reported on issue trackers, and there is no reason not to have this information in the development tools.

From the research point of view this dissertation brought a confirmation of an importance of static analysis, identified strengths and weaknesses of a live quality feedback, highlighted the importance of clear reasoning about false positives, pioneered a 3D decomposition of a quality evolution, discussed the approach to simplify static analysis integration into various tools, and suggested an approach to combat the deficiencies of the modern code review tools. From the engineering point of view during the course of this thesis we updated a few development tools with static analysis feedback and implemented a model of code quality. Our contributions are used by Pharo developers in their daily work. From the ideological point of view we brought the concept of quality-aware tooling to the Pharo community and there is a chance that this concept will continue evolving as developers try to solve their problems with it.

7.5 Closing Words

Software quality is shaped by many aspects. Most of them cannot be easily assessed by simply reading, compiling and executing source code. Various practices and tools emerged over the last years aiming to ensure a good quality of software. However, they are rarely used in practice and thus quality of many software projects is compromised.

In this dissertation we demonstrated that the same tools that are used to create software can assist developers to maintain a good quality by employing the power of static analysis. Based on our experience, live quality feedback combined with customizability of the underlying analysis is a crucial part of software quality assurance.

Appendices

 # The "Missing Yourself" Rule

One of the most infamous rules available in Pharo was named: "*Probably missing '; yourself*' ". The rule detected cascading messages (also known as *cascades*) that did not end with the yourself message although their return value was used in the code. Cascades are a concept specific to Smalltalk and a real example of a message cascade taken from Pharo source code is presented in Listing A.1. On the first line an instance of ToolDockingBarMorph is created. The rest of the lines separated by semicolons contain message sends to the same object (the newly created instance). This construct is very useful for initializing newly created objects with desired values and not having to retype the variable name each time in front of a message. However, the result of the whole cascade expression is equal to the value returned by the last message in the cascade (in our case yourself). This means that if adoptMenuModel: would be the last message and would return an adopted model the whole expression would return it, while the desired result is the instance of

```
1  ^ ToolDockingBarMorph new
2      hResizing: #shrinkWrap;
3      vResizing: #spaceFill;
4      adoptMenuModel: aModel;
5      yourself
```

Listing A.1: Smalltalk cascade example.

`ToolDockingBarMorph`. To avoid this kind of problem, the "*missing yourself*" rule suggests to end cascades with the `yourself` message as shown in the example. This message simply returns the receiver *i.e.*, the the instance of `ToolDockingBarMorph` in our example. This rule can provide useful suggestions for novices who are not aware about the pitfalls of Smalltalk cascades, and it can be absolutely annoying for experienced developers who want a different last message on purpose.

Developers who use the Roassal visualization framework [Bergel 2016], often use the last message of a cascade to create elements of a shape or to apply a normalizer or a builder to their elements. The code in Listing A.2 illustrates one of such cases. On the first line an instance of the `RTBox` shape is created. On lines 2-4 the shape is initialized with required properties. Finally, on the fifth line the message `elementsOn:` will be sent to the shape instance which will return a collection of elements created based on the parameter passed with the message. While this is a completely valid code, the rule would complain, because the cascade's result is assigned to the `elements` variable, and the cascade does not end with `yourself`. For many developers this warning is annoying because their code works completely fine, nevertheless a minority of developers believe that the rule's suggestion is correct. The code from Listing A.2 can be refactored as shown in Listing A.3. This way it is clearer where the shape is created, and when it is used to build elements.

```
1  elements := RTBox new
2      color: Color lightRed;
3      width: [ :cls | cls numberOfVariables * 8 ];
4      height: #numberOfMethods;
5      elementsOn: RTShape withAllSubclasses.
```

Listing A.2: Roassal elements creation with the last cascade message.

```
1  shape := RTBox new
2      color: Color lightRed;
3      width: [ :cls | cls numberOfVariables * 8 ];
4      height: #numberOfMethods;
5      yourself.
6  elements := shape elementsOn: RTShape withAllSubclasses.
```

Listing A.3: Roassal elements creation that does not violate the "missing yourself" rule.

Additional Plugins of QualityAssistant

QualityAssistant is a live static analysis feedback plugin integrated into the main code editor of the Pharo IDE. We discussed it in chapter 4 together with the related evaluations. However, since its release QualityAssistant also provides plugins for the Inspector and Spotter tools [Chiş 2016]. For a long time already the plugins are disabled by default. Originally the plugins were created as the first demonstration of the Renraku model and evaluated together with the main code editor plugin. We believe that the Inspector and Spotter plugins may prove useful in the future

Inspector is a tool that allows developers to inspect objects in Pharo. Objects may have various representations, and a user can select an object from a presentation and inspect it. This enables continuous inspection of objects which is useful during software development. In Pharo everything is an object, including methods and classes. This allowed us to create a special inspector presentation for method and class objects which displays critiques about them. Moreover developers can select and inspect a critique to obtain more information about it. Figure B.1 depicts an inspector open on a method. The critiques presentation (on the left) lists existing violations. Each violation can be followed up by clicking on it and inspecting it in the next pane (on the right) which shows the problematic source code, explanation of the issue, and custom extensions provided by the inspected critique.

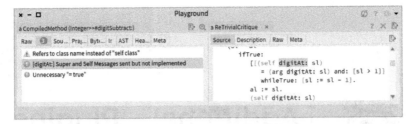

Figure B.1: Code critiques embedded into Pharo Inspector.

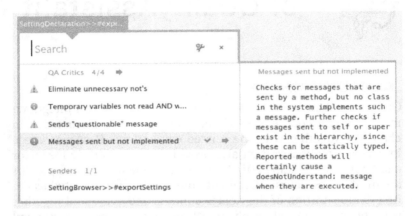

Figure B.2: Code critiques embedded into Pharo Spotter.

Pharo Spotter is a unified search interface that spans many scopes. One can use Spotter to search for tools, or to search for a class, dive into a class to see its components (*e.g.*, methods) and perform a search among these components. Because Spotter allows developers to create various extensions, QualityAssistant adds critiques as components of a class or method. This way if a developer dives into a method or a class, he sees related critiques and can search through them as shown in Figure B.2.

During the survey described in section 4.2 we also asked the participants to evaluate the Inspector and Spotter extensions that were integrated together with QualityAssistant on a 5-point Likert scale from useful to distracting. The results of this assessment are shown in Figure B.3. A bit more than a third of the developers did

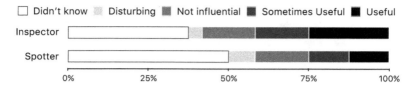

Figure B.3: Usefulness of the other QualityAssistant plugins.

not know about the existence of the Inspector extension, and half of the developers did not know about the Spotter one. We believe that this is caused by the rare usage of Inspector and Spotter to analyze source code entities such as methods. Out of those participants who know about extensions, only half found them useful to some extent.

The Spotter and Inspector plugins were originally packaged with QualityAssistant to show the flexibility of Renraku model that can be used by various tools. The plugins never became popular among developers and ended up being disabled by default. We believe that the plugins may draw more attention in the future, if developers will use Renraku to perform analysis on objects other than classes and methods. At the moment the inspector plugin is useful for developers who design sophisticated custom critiques as they can easily obtain a critique and investigate it in the greater detail. For example while developing the stack critiques that were discussed in subsection 6.1.4, the developer could inspect a stack and explore the critiques that his analyzer produced. Until now there were no use cases where the Spotter plugin was proven to be useful.

Bibliography

[Aniche et al. 2016]   M. ANICHE, G. BAVOTA, C. TREUDE, A. V.DEURSEN, M. A.GEROSA: A Validated Set of Smells in Model-View-Controller Architectures. *In 2016 IEEE International Conference on Software Maintenance and Evolution (ICSME)*, October 2016, S. 233–243

[Ayewah and Pugh 2008]   Nathaniel AYEWAH, William PUGH: A Report on a Survey and Study of Static Analysis Users. *In Proceedings of the 2008 Workshop on Defects in Large Software Systems*. New York, NY, USA : ACM, 2008 (DEFECTS '08), S. 1–5. – URL http://doi.acm.org/10.1145/1390817.1390819. – ISBN 978-1-60558-051-7

[Ayewah and Pugh 2010]   Nathaniel AYEWAH, William PUGH: The Google FindBugs Fixit. *In Proceedings of the 19th International Symposium on Software Testing and Analysis*. New York, NY, USA : ACM, 2010 (ISSTA '10), S. 241–252. – URL http://doi.acm.org/10.1145/1831708.1831738. – ISBN 978-1-60558-823-0

[Ayewah et al. 2007]   Nathaniel AYEWAH, William PUGH, J. D.MORGENTHALER, John PENIX, YuQian ZHOU: Using Find-Bugs on Production Software. *In Companion to the 22Nd ACM SIGPLAN Conference on Object-oriented Programming Systems and Applications Companion*. New York, NY, USA : ACM, 2007 (OOPSLA '07), S. 805–806. – URL http://doi.acm.org/10.1145/1297846.1297897. – ISBN 978-1-59593-865-7

[Bacchelli and Bird 2013]   Alberto BACCHELLI, Christian BIRD: Expectations, Outcomes, and Challenges of Modern Code Review. *In Proceedings of the 2013 International Conference on Software Engineering*. Piscataway, NJ, USA : IEEE Press, 2013 (ICSE '13), S. 712–721. – URL http://dl.acm.org/citation.cfm?id=2486788.2486882. – ISBN 978-1-4673-3076-3

[Bach et al. 2015]   B. BACH, N. HENRY-RICHE, T. DWYER, T. MADHYASTHA, J-D. FEKETE, T. GRABOWSKI: Small MultiPiles: Piling

Time to Explore Temporal Patterns in Dynamic Networks. *In Computer Graphics Forum* 34 (2015), Nr. 3, S. 31–40. – URL http://dx.doi.org/10.1111/cgf.12615. – ISSN 1467-8659

[Bach et al. 2014]   Benjamin BACH, Emmanuel PIETRIGA, Jean-Daniel FEKETE: Visualizing Dynamic Networks with Matrix Cubes. *In Proceedings of the SIGCHI Conference on Human Factors in Computing Systems.* New York, NY, USA : ACM, 2014 (CHI '14), S. 877–886. – URL http://doi.acm.org/10.1145/2556288.2557010. – ISBN 978-1-4503-2473-1

[Balachandran 2013]   Vipin BALACHANDRAN: Reducing human effort and improving quality in peer code reviews using automatic static analysis and reviewer recommendation. *In ICSE'13: Proceedings of 35th International Conference on Software Engineering,* May 2013, S. 931–940. – ISSN 0270-5257

[Ball 1999]   Thomas BALL: The Concept of Dynamic Analysis. *In Proceedings of the European Software Engineering Conference and ACM SIGSOFT International Symposium on the Foundations of Software Engineering (ESEC/FSC'99).* Heidelberg : Springer Verlag, sep 1999 (LNCS 1687), S. 216–234

[Barik et al. 2016]   T. BARIK, Y. SONG, B. JOHNSON, E. MURPHY-HILL: From Quick Fixes to Slow Fixes: Reimagining Static Analysis Resolutions to Enable Design Space Exploration. *In 32nd IEEE International Conference on Software Maintenance and Evolution (ICSME 2016),* October 2016, S. 211–221

[Beck 1997]   Kent BECK: *Smalltalk Best Practice Patterns.* Prentice-Hall, 1997. – URL http://stephane.ducasse.free.fr/FreeBooks/BestSmalltalkPractices/Draft-Smalltalk%20Best%20Practice%20Patterns%20Kent%20Beck.pdf

[Beller et al. 2016]   M. BELLER, R. BHOLANATH, S. MCINTOSH, A. ZAIDMAN: Analyzing the State of Static Analysis: A Large-Scale Evaluation in Open Source Software. *In 2016 IEEE 23rd International Conference on Software Analysis, Evolution, and Reengineering (SANER)* Bd. 1, March 2016, S. 470–481

[Bergel 2016]   A. BERGEL: *Agile Visualization*. LULU Press, 2016.
– URL https://books.google.ch/books?id=lEk7vgAACAAJ. –
ISBN 9781365314094

[Bessey et al. 2010]   Al BESSEY, Ken BLOCK, Ben CHELF, Andy
CHOU, Bryan FULTON, Seth HALLEM, Charles HENRI-GROS, Asya
KAMSKY, Scott MCPEAK, Dawson ENGLER: A few billion lines of
code later: using static analysis to find bugs in the real world. *In
Commun. ACM* 53 (2010), February, Nr. 2, S. 66–75. – URL http:
//doi.acm.org/10.1145/1646353.1646374. – ISSN 0001-0782

[Black et al. 2007]   Andrew BLACK, Stéphane DUCASSE, Oscar
NIERSTRASZ, Damien POLLET, Damien CASSOU, Marcus DENKER:
Squeak by Example. Square Bracket Associates, 2007. – URL
http://SqueakByExample.org/index.html. – http://squeak-
byexample.org. – ISBN 978-3-9523341-0-2

[Boehm et al. 1976]   B. W.BOEHM, J. R.BROWN, M. LIPOW: Quan-
titative Evaluation of Software Quality. *In Proceedings of 2nd
International Conference on Software Engineering*, IEEE Computer
Society Press, 1976, S. 592 – 605

[Bouraqadi et al. 1998]   Noury BOURAQADI, Thomas LEDOUX,
Fred RIVARD: Safe Metaclass Programming. *In Proceedings OOP-
SLA '98*, 1998, S. 84–96

[Brandes and Nick 2011]   U. BRANDES, B. NICK: Asymmetric
Relations in Longitudinal Social Networks. *In IEEE Transactions
on Visualization and Computer Graphics* 17 (2011), December,
Nr. 12, S. 2283–2290

[Brandes et al. 2013]   Ulrik BRANDES, Bobo NICK, Brigitte ROCK-
STROH, Astrid STEFFEN: Gestaltlines. *In Computer Graphics Forum*
32 (2013), Nr. 3pt2, S. 171–180. – URL http://dx.doi.org/10.
1111/cgf.12104

[Brooks 1987]   Frederick P.BROOKS: No Silver Bullet. *In IEEE
Computer* 20 (1987), April, Nr. 4, S. 10–19

[Brooks 1995]   Frederik P.BROOKS: *The Mythical Man-Month*. 2nd.
Reading, Mass. : Addison Wesley Longman, 1995

[Brown et al. 1998]   William J.BROWN, Raphael C.MALVEAU, Hays W.MCCORMICK, Thomas J.MOWBRAY: *AntiPatterns: Refactoring Software, Architectures, and Projects in Crisis.* John Wiley Press, 1998. – ISBN 0-471-19713-0

[Brühlmann 2008]   Andrea BRÜHLMANN: *Enriching Reverse Engineering with Annotations*, University of Bern, Master's thesis, April 2008. – URL http://scg.unibe.ch/archive/masters/Brue08a.pdf

[Buckers et al. 2017]   Tim BUCKERS, Clinton CAO, Michiel DOESBURG, Boning GONG, Sunwei WANG, Moritz BELLER, Andy ZAIDMAN: UAV: Warnings from Multiple Automated Static Analysis Tools at a Glance. *In 2017 IEEE 24th International Conference on Software Analysis, Evolution, and Reengineering (SANER)*, 2017, S. 472–476

[Calcagno et al. 2015]   Cristiano CALCAGNO, Dino DISTEFANO, Jeremy DUBREIL, Dominik GABI, Pieter HOOIMEIJER, Martino LUCA, Peter O'HEARN, Irene PAPAKONSTANTINOU, Jim PURBRICK, Dulma RODRIGUEZ: *Moving Fast with Software Verification.* S. 3–11. *In NFM'15: Proceedings of the 7th NASA Formal Methods International Symposium*, Springer International Publishing, April 2015. – URL http://dx.doi.org/10.1007/978-3-319-17524-9_1. – ISBN 978-3-319-17524-9

[Campbell and Papapetrou 2013]   G. A.CAMPBELL, Patroklos P.PAPAPETROU: *SonarQube in Action.* 1st. Greenwich, CT, USA : Manning Publications Co., 2013. – ISBN 1617290955, 9781617290954

[Chen et al. 2014]   Tse-Hsun CHEN, Weiyi SHANG, Zhen M.JIANG, Ahmed E.HASSAN, Mohamed NASSER, Parminder FLORA: Detecting Performance Anti-patterns for Applications Developed Using Object-relational Mapping. *In Proceedings of the 36th International Conference on Software Engineering.* New York, NY, USA : ACM, 2014 (ICSE 2014), S. 1001–1012. – URL http://doi.acm.org/10.1145/2568225.2568259. – ISBN 978-1-4503-2756-5

[Chiş 2016]   Andrei CHIŞ: *Moldable Tools*, University of Bern, PhD thesis, September 2016. – URL http://scg.unibe.ch/archive/phd/chis-phd.pdf

[Cohen et al. 2006a]   Jason COHEN, Eric BROWN, Brandon DURETTE, Steven TELEKI: *Best kept secrets of peer code review.* Smart Bear, 2006

[Cohen et al. 2006b]   Tal COHEN, Joseph (.GIL, Itay MAMAN: JTL: the Java tools language. *In OOPSLA '06: Proceedings of the 21st annual ACM SIGPLAN conference on Object-oriented programming languages, systems, and applications.* New York, NY, USA : ACM Press, 2006, S. 89–108. – ISBN 1-59593-348-4

[Creswell and Vicki 2006]   John W.CRESWELL, VICKI: *Designing and Conducting Mixed Methods Research.* 1. Sage Publications, Inc, August 2006. – URL http://www.worldcat.org/isbn/1412927927. – ISBN 9781412927925

[De Roover et al. 2011]   Coen DE ROOVER, Carlos NOGUERA, Andy KELLENS, Vivane JONCKERS: The SOUL Tool Suite for Querying Programs in Symbiosis with Eclipse. *In Proceedings of the 9th International Conference on Principles and Practice of Programming in Java.* New York, NY, USA : ACM, 2011 (PPPJ '11), S. 71–80. – URL http://doi.acm.org/10.1145/2093157.2093168. – ISBN 978-1-4503-0935-6

[Do et al. 2016]   Lisa Nguyen Q.DO, Karim ALI, Benjamin LIVSHITS, Eric BODDEN, Justin SMITH, Emerson MURPHY-HILL, IEM FRAUNHOFER: Just-in-Time Static Analysis / University of Alberta. August 2016. – Forschungsbericht

[Ducasse et al. 2017]   Stéphane DUCASSE, Dmitri ZAGIDULIN, Nicolai HESS, Dimitris CHLOUPIS: *Pharo by Example 5.0.* Square Bracket Associates, 2017. – URL http://files.pharo.org/books/updated-pharo-by-example/. – ISBN 978-1-365-65459-6

[Dustin et al. 1999]   Elfriede DUSTIN, Jeff RASHKA, John PAUL: *Automated Software Testing: Introduction, Management, and Performance.* Boston, MA, USA : Addison-Wesley Longman Publishing Co., Inc., 1999. – ISBN 0-201-43287-0

[Duvall et al. 2007]   Paul DUVALL, Stephen M.MATYAS, Andrew GLOVER: *Continuous Integration: Improving Software Quality and*

Reducing Risk (The Addison-Wesley Signature Series). Addison-Wesley Professional, 2007. – ISBN 0321336380

[Ens et al. 2014]   B. ENS, D. REA, R. SHPANER, H. HEMMATI, J. E.YOUNG, P. IRANI: ChronoTwigger: A Visual Analytics Tool for Understanding Source and Test Co-evolution. *In Proceedings of the VISSOFT '14 Second IEEE Working Conference on Software Visualization*, September 2014, S. 117–126

[Fagan 1976]   Mike FAGAN: Design and code inspections to reduce errors in program development. *In IBM Journal of Research and Development* 15 (1976), Nr. 3, S. 182

[Fowler et al. 1999]   Martin FOWLER, Kent BECK, John BRANT, William OPDYKE, Don ROBERTS: *Refactoring: Improving the Design of Existing Code*. Addison Wesley, 1999

[Gamma et al. 1995]   Erich GAMMA, Richard HELM, Ralph JOHNSON, John VLISSIDES: *Design Patterns: Elements of Reusable Object-Oriented Software*. Reading, Mass. : Addison Wesley Professional, 1995. – ISBN 978-0201633610

[Ganea et al. 2017]   George GANEA, Ioana VEREBI, Radu MARINESCU: Continuous quality assessment with inCode. *In Science of Computer Programming*   134 (2017), S. 19–36. – URL http://www.sciencedirect.com/science/article/pii/S0167642315000520. – Zugriffsdatum: 2017-08-09. – ISSN 0167-6423

[Goldberg and Robson 1983]   Adele GOLDBERG, David ROBSON: *Smalltalk 80: the Language and its Implementation*. Reading, Mass. : Addison Wesley, May 1983. – URL http://stephane.ducasse.free.fr/FreeBooks/BlueBook/Bluebook.pdf. – ISBN 0-201-13688-0

[Gómez et al. 2010]   Verónica U.GÓMEZ, Stéphane DUCASSE, Theo D'HONDT: Visually Supporting Source Code Changes Integration: The Torch Dashboard. *In WCRE'10: Proceedings of the 17th International Working Conference on Reverse Engineering*. Beverly, MA, USA : IEEE Computer Society, October 2010, S. 55–64. – ISSN 1095-1350

[Hao et al. 2013]   Yiyang HAO, Ge LI, Lili MOU, Lu ZHANG, Zhi JIN: MCT: A Tool for Commenting Programs by Multimedia Comments. *In Proceedings of the 2013 International Conference on Software Engineering.* Piscataway, NJ, USA : IEEE Press, 2013 (ICSE '13), S. 1339–1342. – URL http://dl.acm.org/citation.cfm?id=2486788.2487000. – ISBN 978-1-4673-3076-3

[Harrison 2006]   W. HARRISON: Eating Your Own Dog Food. *In IEEE Software* 23 (2006), May, Nr. 3, S. 5–7. – ISSN 0740-7459

[Hecht et al. 2015]   G. HECHT, R. ROUVOY, N. MOHA, L. DUCHIEN: Detecting Antipatterns in Android Apps. *In 2015 2nd ACM International Conference on Mobile Software Engineering and Systems,* May 2015, S. 148–149

[Heckman and Williams 2008]   Sarah HECKMAN, Laurie WILLIAMS: On Establishing a Benchmark for Evaluating Static Analysis Alert Prioritization and Classification Techniques. *In Proceedings of the Second ACM-IEEE International Symposium on Empirical Software Engineering and Measurement.* New York, NY, USA : ACM, 2008 (ESEM '08), S. 41–50. – URL http://doi.acm.org/10.1145/1414004.1414013. – ISBN 978-1-59593-971-5

[Hora et al. 2012]   A. HORA, N. ANQUETIL, S. DUCASSE, S. ALLIER: Domain specific warnings: Are they any better? *In 2012 28th IEEE International Conference on Software Maintenance (ICSM),* September 2012, S. 441–450. – ISSN 1063-6773

[ISO/IEC 2010]   ISO/IEC: *ISO/IEC 25010 — Systems and software engineering — Systems and software Quality Requirements and Evaluation (SQuaRE) — System and software quality models.* 2010

[Johnson et al. 2013]   Brittany JOHNSON, Yoonki SONG, Emerson MURPHY-HILL, Robert BOWDIDGE: Why Don't Software Developers Use Static Analysis Tools to Find Bugs? *In Proceedings of the 2013 International Conference on Software Engineering,* IEEE Press, 2013 (ICSE '13), S. 672–681. – URL http://dl.acm.org/citation.cfm?id=2486788.2486877. – ISBN 978-1-4673-3076-3

[Johnson 1978]   S.C. JOHNSON: Lint, a C Program Checker. *In UNIX programmer's manual*. AT&T Bell Laboratories, 1978, S. 78–1273

[Keim and Kriegel 1996]   Daniel A.KEIM, H-P KRIEGEL: Visualization techniques for mining large databases: A comparison. *In Knowledge and Data Engineering, IEEE Transactions on* 8 (1996), Nr. 6, S. 923–938

[Khomh et al. 2009]   Foutse KHOMH, Massimiliano DI PENTA, Yann-Gael GUEHENEUC: An Exploratory Study of the Impact of Code Smells on Software Change-proneness. *In Proceedings of the 2009 16th Working Conference on Reverse Engineering*. Washington, DC, USA : IEEE Computer Society, 2009 (WCRE '09), S. 75–84. – URL http://dx.doi.org/10.1109/WCRE.2009.28. – ISBN 978-0-7695-3867-9

[King et al. 1999]   Peter KING, Patrick NAUGHTON, Mike DE-MONEY, Jonni KANERVA, Kathy WALRATH, Scott HOMMEL: *Java Code Conventions*. Sun Microsystems Inc, 1999

[Lanza and Ducasse 2002]   Michele LANZA, Stéphane DUCASSE: Understanding Software Evolution Using a Combination of Software Visualization and Software Metrics. *In Proceedings of Langages et Modèles à Objets (LMO'02)*. Paris : Lavoisier, 2002, S. 135–149. – URL http://scg.unibe.ch/archive/papers/Lanz02aEvolutionMatrix.pdf

[Lanza and Marinescu 2006]   Michele LANZA, Radu MARINESCU: *Object-Oriented Metrics in Practice*. Springer-Verlag, 2006. – URL http://www.springer.com/de/book/9783540244295. – ISBN 3-540-24429-8

[Louridas 2006]   Panagiotis LOURIDAS: Static Code Analysis. *In IEEE Softw.* 23 (2006), July, Nr. 4, S. 58–61. – URL http://dx.doi.org/10.1109/MS.2006.114. – ISSN 0740-7459

[Lozano et al. 2015]   Angela LOZANO, Kim MENS, Andy KELLENS: Usage contracts: Offering immediate feedback on violations of structural source-code regularities.   *In Science of Computer Programming*   105 (2015), S. 73 – 91.

– URL http://www.sciencedirect.com/science/article/pii/S016764231500012X. – ISSN 0167-6423

[Lungu 2009]   Mircea LUNGU: *Reverse Engineering Software Ecosystems*, University of Lugano, Dissertation, November 2009. – URL http://scg.unibe.ch/archive/papers/Lung09b.pdf

[Maletic et al. 2002]   Jonathan I.MALETIC, Andrian MARCUS, Michael COLLARD: A Task Oriented View of Software Visualization. *In Proceedings of the 1st Workshop on Visualizing Software for Understanding and Analysis (VISSOFT 2002)*, IEEE, June 2002, S. 32–40

[Marcus et al. 2003]   Andrian MARCUS, Louis FENG, Jonathan I.MALETIC: 3D Representations for Software Visualization. *In Proceedings of the ACM Symposium on Software Visualization*, IEEE, 2003, S. 27–ff

[Marinescu 2004]   Radu MARINESCU: Detection Strategies: Metrics-Based Rules for Detecting Design Flaws. *In 20th IEEE International Conference on Software Maintenance (ICSM'04)*. Los Alamitos CA : IEEE Computer Society Press, 2004, S. 350–359

[Mazinanian et al. 2014]   Davood MAZINANIAN, Nikolaos TSANTALIS, Ali MESBAH: Discovering Refactoring Opportunities in Cascading Style Sheets. *In Proceedings of the 22Nd ACM SIGSOFT International Symposium on Foundations of Software Engineering*. New York, NY, USA : ACM, 2014 (FSE 2014), S. 496–506. – URL http://doi.acm.org/10.1145/2635868.2635879. – ISBN 978-1-4503-3056-5

[Merino et al. 2017]   Leonel MERINO, Mohammad GHAFARI, Craig ANSLOW, Oscar NIERSTRASZ: CityVR: Gameful Software Visualization. *In ICSME'17: Proceedings of the 33rd IEEE International Conference on Software Maintenance and Evolution (TD Track)*, IEEE, 2017. – URL http://scg.unibe.ch/archive/papers/Meri17c.pdf. – To appear

[Minelli et al. 2014]   R. MINELLI, L. BARACCHI, A. MOCCI, M. LANZA: Visual Storytelling of Development Sessions. *In 2014 IEEE International Conference on Software Maintenance and Evolution*, September 2014, S. 416–420. – ISSN 1063-6773

[Moha et al. 2010]   N. MOHA, Y. G.GUEHENEUC, L. DUCHIEN, A. F. L.MEUR: DECOR: A Method for the Specification and Detection of Code and Design Smells. *In IEEE Transactions on Software Engineering* 36 (2010), January, Nr. 1, S. 20–36. – ISSN 0098-5589

[Muske and Serebrenik 2016]   Tukaram MUSKE, Alexander SEREBRENIK: Survey of Approaches for Handling Static Analysis Alarms. *In 2016 IEEE 16th International Working Conference on Source Code Analysis and Manipulation (SCAM)*, October 2016, S. 157–166

[Oppenheim 2000]   Abraham N.OPPENHEIM: *Questionnaire design, interviewing and attitude measurement.* Bloomsbury Publishing, 2000. – ISBN 9780826451767

[Palomba et al. 2014]   F. PALOMBA, G. BAVOTA, M. D.PENTA, R. OLIVETO, A. D.LUCIA: Do They Really Smell Bad? A Study on Developers' Perception of Bad Code Smells. *In 2014 IEEE International Conference on Software Maintenance and Evolution*, September 2014, S. 101–110. – ISSN 1063-6773

[Palsberg   and   Schwartzbach   1991]   Jens   PALSBERG, Michael I.SCHWARTZBACH: Object-Oriented Type Inference. *In Proceedings OOPSLA '91, ACM SIGPLAN Notices* Bd. 26, URL http://www.cs.purdue.edu/homes/palsberg/publications.html, November 1991, S. 146–161

[ParcPlace98 1998]   *VisualWorks 3.0 Application Developer's Guide.* 1998. – ParcPlace Division

[Renggli et al. 2010a]   Lukas RENGGLI, Stéphane DUCASSE, Tudor GÎRBA, Oscar NIERSTRASZ: Domain-Specific Program Checking. *In Proceedings of the 48th International Conference on Objects, Models, Components and Patterns (TOOLS'10)* Bd. 6141, Springer-Verlag, 2010, S. 213–232. –   URL http://scg.unibe.ch/archive/papers/Reng10bDomainSpecificProgramChecking.pdf

[Renggli et al. 2010b]   Lukas RENGGLI, Tudor GÎRBA, Oscar NIERSTRASZ: Embedding Languages Without Breaking Tools. *In ECOOP'10: Proceedings of the 24th European Conference on Object-Oriented Programming* Bd. 6183. Maribor, Slovenia : Springer-Verlag, 2010, S. 380–404. –   URL http://scg.unibe.ch/

archive/papers/Reng10aEmbeddingLanguages.pdf. – ISBN 978-3-642-14106-5

[Riel 1996]   Arthur RIEL: *Object-Oriented Design Heuristics*. Boston MA : Addison Wesley, 1996. – 400 S

[Rigby and Bird 2013]   Peter C.RIGBY, Christian BIRD: Convergent Contemporary Software Peer Review Practices. *In Proceedings of the 2013 9th Joint Meeting on Foundations of Software Engineering*. New York, NY, USA : ACM, 2013 (ESEC/FSE 2013), S. 202–212. – URL http://doi.acm.org/10.1145/2491411.2491444. – ISBN 978-1-4503-2237-9

[Roberts et al. 1997]   Don ROBERTS, John BRANT, Ralph E.JOHNSON: A Refactoring Tool for Smalltalk. *In Theory and Practice of Object Systems (TAPOS)* 3 (1997), Nr. 4, S. 253–263

[Roberts et al. 1996]   Don ROBERTS, John BRANT, Ralph E.JOHNSON, Bill OPDYKE: An Automated Refactoring Tool. *In Proceedings of ICAST '96, Chicago, IL*, April 1996

[Roberts 1999]   Donald B.ROBERTS: *Practical Analysis for Refactoring*, University of Illinois, Dissertation, 1999. – URL http://historical.ncstrl.org/tr/pdf/uiuc_cs/UIUCDCS-R-99-2092.pdf

[Roehm et al. 2012]   Tobias ROEHM, Rebecca TIARKS, Rainer KOSCHKE, Walid MAALEJ: How do professional developers comprehend software? *In Proceedings of the 2012 International Conference on Software Engineering*. Piscataway, NJ, USA : IEEE Press, 2012 (ICSE 2012), S. 255–265. – ISBN 978-1-4673-1067-3

[Rufiange and Melançon 2014]   S. RUFIANGE, G. MELANÇON: AniMatrix: A Matrix-Based Visualization of Software Evolution. *In Software Visualization (VISSOFT), 2014 Second IEEE Working Conference on*, September 2014, S. 137–146

[Sadowski et al. 2015]   Caitlin SADOWSKI, Jeffrey van GOGH, Ciera JASPAN, Emma SÖDERBERG, Collin WINTER: Tricorder: Building a Program Analysis Ecosystem. *In Proceedings of the*

37th International Conference on Software Engineering - Volume 1. Piscataway, NJ, USA : IEEE Press, 2015 (ICSE '15), S. 598–608. – URL http://dl.acm.org/citation.cfm?id=2818754.2818828. – ISBN 978-1-4799-1934-5

[Schärli et al. 2002]   Nathanael SCHÄRLI, Stéphane DUCASSE, Oscar NIERSTRASZ, Andrew P.BLACK: Traits: Composable Units of Behavior / Institut für Informatik. Universität Bern, Switzerland, November 2002 (IAM-02-005). – Technical Report. – URL http://scg.unibe.ch/archive/papers/Scha02bTraits.pdf. Also available as Technical Report CSE-02-014, OGI School of Science & Engineering, Beaverton, Oregon, USA

[Sheridan 2012]   Flash SHERIDAN: Deploying Static Analysis. *In Dr. Dobb's Journal* (2012), August, S. 8–14. – URL http://www.rahul.net/flash/Deploying_Static_Analysis.pdf. – ISSN 1066-8888

[Shneiderman 1996]   Ben SHNEIDERMAN: The Eyes Have It: A Task by Data Type Taxonomy for Information Visualizations. *In IEEE Visual Languages.* College Park, Maryland 20742, U.S.A., 1996, S. 336–343

[Singer et al. 1997]   Janice SINGER, Timothy LETHBRIDGE, Norman VINSON, Nicolas ANQUETIL: An examination of software engineering work practices. *In Proceedings of the 1997 conference of the Centre for Advanced Studies on Collaborative research*, IBM Press, 1997 (CASCON '97), S. 21–. – URL http://dl.acm.org/citation.cfm?id=782010.782031

[Stallman 1981]   Richard M.STALLMAN: EMACS the Extensible, Customizable Self-documenting Display Editor. *In ACM SIGOA Newsletter* 2 (1981), April, Nr. 1-2, S. 147–156. – URL http://doi.acm.org/10.1145/1159890.806466. – ISSN 0737-819X

[Tymchuk 2015]   Yuriy TYMCHUK: What if Clippy Would Criticize Your Code? *In BENEVOL'15: Proceedings of the 14th edition of the Belgian-Netherlands software evoLution seminar*, URL http://yuriy.tymch.uk/papers/benevol15.pdf, December 2015

[Tymchuk 2017a] Yuriy TYMCHUK: The False False Positives of Static Analysis. *In SATToSE'17: Pre-Proceedings of the 10th International Seminar Series on Advanced Techniques & Tools for Software Evolution*, URL http://scg.unibe.ch/archive/papers/Tymc17c.pdf, June 2017

[Tymchuk 2017b] Yuriy TYMCHUK: *QualityAssistant Interactions*. August 2017. – URL https://doi.org/10.5281/zenodo.846690

[Tymchuk 2017c] Yuriy TYMCHUK: *QualityAssistant v3.3.1*. June 2017. – URL https://doi.org/10.5281/zenodo.809410

[Tymchuk 2017d] Yuriy TYMCHUK: *Renraku v0.15.2*. May 2017. – URL https://doi.org/10.5281/zenodo.800676

[Tymchuk et al. 2016a] Yuriy TYMCHUK, Mohammad GHAFARI, Oscar NIERSTRASZ: When QualityAssistant Meets Pharo: Enforced Code Critiques Motivate More Valuable Rules. *In IWST '16: Proceedings of International Workshop on Smalltalk Technologies*, URL http://scg.unibe.ch/archive/papers/Tymc16b.pdf, 2016, S. 5:1–5:6

[Tymchuk et al. 2017] Yuriy TYMCHUK, Mohammad GHAFARI, Oscar NIERSTRASZ: Renraku — the One Static Analysis Model to Rule Them All. *In IWST'17: Proceedings of International Workshop on Smalltalk Technologies*, URL http://scg.unibe.ch/archive/papers/Tymc17d.pdf, 2017

[Tymchuk et al. 2016b] Yuriy TYMCHUK, Leonel MERINO, Mohammad GHAFARI, Oscar NIERSTRASZ: *[Artifact] Walls, Pillars and Beams: A 3D Decomposition of Quality Anomalies*. June 2016. – URL https://doi.org/10.5281/zenodo.56111

[Tymchuk et al. 2016c] Yuriy TYMCHUK, Leonel MERINO, Mohammad GHAFARI, Oscar NIERSTRASZ: Walls, Pillars and Beams: A 3D Decomposition of Quality Anomalies. *In VISSOFT'16: Proceedings of the 4th IEEE Working Conference on Software Visualization*, IEEE, 2016, S. 126–135. – URL http://scg.unibe.ch/archive/papers/Tymc16a.pdf

[Tymchuk et al. 2015a]   Yuriy TYMCHUK, Andrea MOCCI, Michele LANZA: Code Review: Veni, ViDI, Vici. *In SANER'15: Proceedings of the 22rd IEEE International Conference on Software Analysis, Evolution, and Reengineering*, IEEE, March 2015, S. 151–160. – URL http://yuriy.tymch.uk/papers/saner15.pdf

[Tymchuk et al. 2015b]   Yuriy TYMCHUK, Andrea MOCCI, Michele LANZA: ViDI: The Visual Design Inspector. *In ICSE'15: Proceedings of the 37th International Conference on Software Engineering, Tool Demonstration* Bd. 2, IEEE, May 2015, S. 653–656. – URL http://yuriy.tymch.uk/papers/icse15.pdf

[Ware 2004]   Colin WARE: *Information Visualisation*. Sansome Street, San Fransico : Elsevier, 2004. – ISBN 1-55860-819-2

[Wettel 2010]   Richard WETTEL: *Software Systems as Cities*, University of Lugano, Switzerland, Dissertation, September 2010

[Woodruff et al. 1998]   Allison WOODRUFF, James LANDAY, Michael STONEBRAKER: Goal-directed zoom. *In CHI 98 conference summary on Human factors in computing systems*. New York, NY, USA : ACM, 1998 (CHI '98), S. 305–306. – ISBN 1-58113-028-7

[Yamashita and Moonen 2013]   Aiko YAMASHITA, Leon MOONEN: Do developers care about code smells? An exploratory survey. *In WCRE'13* (2013), S. 242–251. – ISBN 9781479929313

[Zimmermann and Weißgerber 2004]   Thomas ZIMMERMANN, Peter WEISSGERBER: Preprocessing CVS Data for Fine-Grained Analysis. *In Proceedings 1st International Workshop on Mining Software Repositories (MSR 2004)*. Los Alamitos CA : IEEE Computer Society Press, 2004, S. 2–6

www.ingramcontent.com/pod-product-compliance
Lightning Source LLC
Chambersburg PA
CBHW071117050326
40690CB00008B/1256